WHAT IS THE BOOK OF EXODUS?

Kids' Guides to God's Word Series

What Is the Book of

EXODUS?

Michael Whitworth

START2FINISH

ISBN 978-1-971767-11-6

Published by Start2Finish
Bend, Oregon 97702
start2finish.org

Printed in the United States of America

30 29 28 27 26   1 2 3 4 5

CONTENTS

INTRODUCTION

Have you ever been stuck somewhere you didn't want to be? Maybe it was in a class that felt endless, a family situation that seemed impossible, or a season of life where you just wanted out. You could see what freedom might look like, but you couldn't get there. Something was holding you back—circumstances, other people, your own limitations. And you wondered if things would ever change.

Now multiply that feeling by four hundred years. That's how long the Israelites were stuck in Egypt. What started as a refuge during a famine became a prison. The family of seventy that moved there to survive grew into a nation of millions—and the Egyptians forced them into brutal slavery. Generation after generation was born into chains. They made bricks. They built cities. They suffered under the whip. And they cried out to a God they weren't sure was listening.

The book of Exodus is the story of how God answered. It's a story of plagues and miracles, of seas parting and mountains shaking. It's the story of the most famous confrontation in the Bible—an unknown shepherd versus the most powerful king on earth. It's the story of how a nation of slaves became the people of God.

But it's more than ancient history. Exodus is the Bible's foundational story of salvation. Everything that comes later—the prophets, the psalms, the promises of a Messiah—looks back to what God did in Egypt. And when Jesus came, he didn't come to tell a new story. He came to finish this one.

If you want to understand the Bible, you have to understand the exodus. This is where it all comes together.

WHERE WE'VE BEEN

Exodus picks up where Genesis left off—but four centuries have passed. At the end of Genesis, Jacob's family moved to Egypt to escape a famine. Joseph, the brother who had been sold into slavery, was now second-in-command of the entire nation. He saved his family, settled them in the best land, and everything seemed fine.

Then Joseph died. And a new pharaoh came to power "who did not know Joseph." That single sentence in Exodus 1 changes everything. The new king didn't remember how a Hebrew had saved Egypt from starvation. He only saw a growing foreign population that might become a threat. So he enslaved them. When slavery didn't slow their growth, he ordered the murder of their baby boys.

For four hundred years, the Israelites suffered. They had God's promises—the same promises he made to Abraham, Isaac, and Jacob—but those promises must have felt impossibly distant. God had said their descendants would be as numerous as the stars and would inherit the land of Canaan. Instead, they were making bricks in Egypt and watching their children die. Had God forgotten them?

WHAT YOU'RE ABOUT TO READ

The book of Exodus answers that question with a thundering no. God had not forgotten. He had heard their cries. He had seen their suffering. And he was about to act in ways that would shake the ancient world and echo through the rest of history.

Here's where we're headed:

Chapters 1–6 set the stage. You'll meet Moses—the baby who should have died but was rescued by Pharaoh's own daughter. You'll watch him grow up in the palace, flee after killing an Egyptian, and spend forty years as a shepherd in the wilderness. Then, at a burning bush that doesn't burn up, God calls him to go back to Egypt and tell Pharaoh to let his people go.

Chapters 7–11 describe the ten plagues. Blood. Frogs. Gnats. Flies. Livestock disease. Boils. Hail. Locusts. Darkness. And finally, the death of every firstborn in Egypt. Each plague was a direct assault on the gods of Egypt, proving that the Lord alone is God. Pharaoh's heart grew harder with each one—until the final plague broke him.

Chapters 12–15 tell the story of the Passover and the exodus itself. The Israelites marked their doorframes with lamb's blood, and the angel of death passed over them. That same night, they walked out of Egypt—free for the first time in four centuries. When Pharaoh changed his mind and sent his army after them, God parted the Red Sea and drowned the Egyptian forces. The nation that had seemed invincible was destroyed in a single night.

Chapters 15–18 follow Israel through the wilderness. Freedom, it turns out, is harder than it looks. The people complained about water, about food, about everything. They faced attacks from enemies. They struggled to trust the God who had just performed miracles before their eyes. But God provided—manna from heaven, water from rock, victory in battle.

Chapters 19–24 bring us to Mount Sinai, where God gave his people the Ten Commandments and established his covenant with them. Thunder rolled. Lightning flashed. The mountain shook. And the voice of God himself spoke the words that would define Israel's relationship with him forever.

Chapters 25–31 and 35–40 describe the tabernacle—the portable dwelling place where God would live among his people. Every detail mattered. Every piece of furniture taught something about approaching a holy God. And when it was finally built, the glory of the Lord filled it so powerfully that even Moses couldn't enter.

Chapters 32–34 tell the devastating story of the golden calf—Israel's greatest failure, coming just weeks after they promised to obey everything God commanded. You'll watch Moses intercede for the people, shatter the stone tablets in anger, and climb the mountain again to receive God's mercy and a renewed covenant.

By the end of Exodus, everything has changed. The slaves are free. The covenant is established. The tabernacle is built. God is dwelling among his people. The exodus is complete.

WHY THIS BOOK MATTERS

You might be thinking, "That's a great story, but it happened thousands of years ago. Why should I care?" Here's why: the exodus isn't just Israel's story. It's a pattern that repeats throughout the Bible—and it's your story too.

The exodus shows us what salvation looks like. Slavery, rescue, covenant, presence. That's the shape of what God does for his people. Israel was enslaved to Egypt; we're enslaved to sin. Israel couldn't free themselves; neither can we. Israel was rescued by blood—the blood of the Passover lamb; we're rescued by blood too—the blood of Jesus, "the Lamb of God who takes away the sin of the world" (John 1:29).

The connections aren't subtle. Jesus died during the Passover festival. The night before his death, he lifted a cup of wine and said, "This is my blood of the covenant" (Matthew 26:28). When the New Testament wants to describe what Jesus accomplished, it reaches for exodus language: redemption, deliverance, freedom, rescue.

The exodus also shows us who God is. A God who hears the cries of the oppressed. A God who keeps promises even when centuries pass. A God who is holy beyond comprehension but wants to dwell among his people. A God who is both terrifying and tender, just and merciful, powerful and patient.

Every page of Exodus reveals something about God's character. Pay attention. What you learn here will shape how you understand everything else in Scripture.

BEFORE YOU BEGIN

A few things to keep in mind as you read:

The story moves at different speeds. The first half of Exodus is fast-paced narrative—plagues, escapes, battles. The second half slows way down to describe the tabernacle in painstaking detail. Both parts matter. The action shows us what God did; the tabernacle shows us why he did it—to live among his people.

The characters are complicated. Moses argues with God. Aaron makes a golden calf. The people complain constantly. The Bible doesn't sanitize its heroes. It shows real people with real failures being used by a real God.

The violence is real. Plagues that killed livestock and children. An army drowned in the sea. Israelites executed for idolatry. Exodus doesn't shy away from the cost of sin or the seriousness of God's judgment. These aren't comfortable passages, but they're honest about the stakes.

This points forward. Everything in Exodus casts a shadow toward something greater. The Passover lamb points to Jesus. The tabernacle points to God dwelling with us in Christ. The covenant points to the new covenant. Moses the deliverer points to the greater Deliverer who was coming.

LET'S BEGIN

So here we are, about to enter one of the most important books ever written. We'll watch a baby in a basket become a prince, a prince become a fugitive, and a fugitive become a deliverer. We'll stand before Pharaoh and watch his empire crumble. We'll walk through the Red Sea on dry ground. We'll tremble at the foot of a smoking mountain. We'll see God's glory fill a tent in the wilderness.

And through it all, we'll learn what it means to be saved—really saved—by a God who hears, who remembers, who acts, and who never lets his people go.

The Israelites were stuck for four hundred years.
Then God showed up.
Turn the page.

1

WHEN EVERYTHING CHANGED

In *The Lion, the Witch and the Wardrobe,* the children step through a magical wardrobe into the land of Narnia—and discover something terrible. Narnia is frozen. The White Witch has ruled for a hundred years, and under her curse, it's always winter and never Christmas. The trees are bare, the rivers are ice, and the creatures who remember the old days live in hiding, whispering about a lion named Aslan who might one day return. But he hasn't come. Not yet. And in the meantime, the Witch's secret police roam the woods, and anyone who resists disappears.

If you walked away from Genesis thinking the story of Israel was heading somewhere good, Exodus 1 is about to shock you. Like Narnia under the Witch, everything has frozen over. The family that went down to Egypt as honored guests has become a nation of slaves. The God who made all those promises? He seems to have gone silent.

Welcome to Exodus. This is where the Bible's greatest rescue story begins.

THE STORY SO FAR

At the end of Genesis, things looked promising. Joseph—the brother sold into slavery—rose to become the second most powerful man in Egypt. When famine struck, he saved his entire family. Pharaoh welcomed Jacob and his sons, giving them the best land in Egypt.

Seventy people went down to Egypt. Just seventy. A tiny family carrying an enormous promise. God had told Abraham his descendants would become a great nation. He had also told Abraham something else: "Know for certain that your descendants will be strangers in a country not their own, and they will be enslaved and mistreated four hundred years" (Genesis 15:13). Four hundred years of slavery. God saw it coming. And now, as Exodus opens, that terrible prophecy is coming true.

A NEW KING WHO DID NOT KNOW JOSEPH

Exodus begins with a list of names—the sons of Jacob who went to Egypt. It's the same list from the end of Genesis. Same family. Same promise. Same God.

But then comes the most dangerous sentence in the chapter: "Then a new king, who did not know about Joseph, came to power in Egypt." Joseph, who saved Egypt from starvation. Joseph, who made Pharaoh wealthy beyond imagination. That Joseph. Forgotten. As if he never existed.

This is what happens when generations pass. The people who remembered Joseph died. And the new Pharaoh looked at the Israelites and saw only one thing: a threat.

"Look," he said, "the Israelites have become far too numerous for us. Come, we must deal shrewdly with them or they will become even more numerous and, if war breaks out, will join our enemies, fight against us and leave the country." Notice what Pharaoh fears. Not that the Israelites will attack. He's afraid they'll *leave*. He wants slaves—and he wants them too broken to dream of freedom.

THE CRUELTY OF EGYPT

So Egypt put slave masters over the Israelites. The Bible uses brutal language: they "oppressed them with forced labor," "worked them ruthlessly," and "made their lives bitter with harsh labor." The Israelites built cities for Pharaoh—Pithom and Rameses. Massive construction projects requiring thousands of workers baking bricks under the scorching sun, hauling heavy loads, mixing mortar until their hands bled.

But here's what Pharaoh didn't expect: "The more they were oppressed, the more they multiplied and spread." Read that again. The more Egypt crushed them, the more the Israelites grew.

God had promised Abraham descendants as numerous as the stars. Even under the worst conditions imaginable, that promise was coming true. The Israelites were "fruitful and multiplied"—the same words from Genesis when God blessed humanity at creation. Despite everything Pharaoh could do, God's blessing could not be stopped.

This terrified the Egyptians. "They came to dread the Israelites." Something more powerful than Pharaoh was at work—and Egypt could feel it.

TWO WOMEN WHO FEARED GOD

Since working the Israelites to death wasn't stopping their growth, Pharaoh tried something darker. He called in the Hebrew midwives and gave them a horrifying order: "When you are helping the Hebrew women during childbirth, if you see that the baby is a boy, kill him; but if it is a girl, let her live." Genocide. State-sponsored murder of baby boys.

But something remarkable happened. The midwives—Shiphrah and Puah—refused to obey. These weren't soldiers or political leaders. They were working-class women living under an absolute dictator who could have them executed for any reason. Pharaoh's word was law. No one told Pharaoh no.

Shiphrah and Puah told Pharaoh no. "The midwives feared God," the Bible says, "and did not do what the king of Egypt had told them to do; they let the boys live." God "was kind to the midwives" and "gave them families of their own." In a book full of powerful men trying to control history, the first heroes are two ordinary women who trusted God more than they feared a king.

INTO THE NILE

Pharaoh's plan had failed. So he escalated. "Then Pharaoh gave this order to all his people: 'Every Hebrew boy that is born you must throw into the Nile, but let every girl live.'"

This wasn't a secret order anymore. Any Egyptian who saw a Hebrew baby boy was supposed to throw him into the river. The Nile—Egypt's lifeblood—was to become a grave for Israelite children.

This is the world Moses is about to be born into.

A BABY IN A BASKET

Exodus 2 opens simply: "A man of the tribe of Levi married a Levite woman, and she became pregnant and gave birth to a son." This boy was born with a death sentence over him. Every Egyptian had permission to throw him into the Nile.

His mother "saw that he was a fine child" and couldn't let him die. For three months, she hid him. But babies grow. They get louder.

So she did something that took incredible faith. She got a papyrus basket, coated it with tar to make it waterproof, placed her baby inside, and set it among the reeds along the Nile.

Pharaoh had commanded Hebrew boys be thrown into the Nile. In a sense, that's what this mother did—she put her baby in the Nile. But she did it in a way that gave him a chance. She built him a tiny ark (the same word used for Noah's ark) and trusted God with the rest. His sister stood at a distance to watch.

PHARAOH'S DAUGHTER

What happened next could only be God. Pharaoh's daughter came down to bathe. She saw the basket and sent her slave to get it. When she opened it, she saw the baby crying. "This is one of the Hebrew babies," she said. She knew. A child marked for death by her own father's decree. She could have followed the law. But she felt sorry for him. And everything changed.

The baby's sister appeared and asked, "Shall I go and get one of the Hebrew women to nurse the baby for you?" Pharaoh's daughter agreed. The sister ran and got the baby's own mother.

Think about the irony. The mother gets paid to nurse her own son. The boy marked for death by Pharaoh ends up raised in Pharaoh's palace. The murderer's daughter becomes the victim's protector.

"When the child grew older, she took him to Pharaoh's daughter and he became her son. She named him Moses, saying, 'I drew him out of the water.'" *Moses.* The name sounds like "draw out." Pharaoh's daughter didn't know it, but she was naming the man who would one day draw an entire nation out of Egypt.

THE PRINCE WHO CHOSE HIS PEOPLE

Moses grew up in Pharaoh's palace with the best education, finest food, finest clothes. By all appearances, he was an Egyptian prince. But he knew who he really was.

"One day, after Moses had grown up, he went out to where his own people were and watched them at their hard labor." *His own people.* Despite the palace and the privilege, Moses knew he belonged to the Hebrews. And when he saw an Egyptian beating a Hebrew slave, something snapped.

He looked around. No one was watching. He killed the Egyptian and hid the body in the sand. This was murder. Moses saw injustice and responded with violence. His heart was right—he cared about his people—but his method was wrong.

The next day, Moses saw two Hebrews fighting. When he intervened, one shot back: "Who made you ruler and judge over us? Are you thinking of killing me as you killed the Egyptian?" Word spread to Pharaoh, who tried to kill Moses. So Moses fled to Midian. Just like that, the prince of Egypt became a fugitive.

FORTY YEARS IN THE WILDERNESS

In Midian, Moses sat down by a well—and immediately got involved in another conflict. Shepherds were driving away women trying to water their flocks. Moses rescued the women and helped water their animals.

Even in exile, Moses couldn't ignore injustice.

The women were daughters of a priest named Reuel (also called Jethro). Moses eventually married one of them, Zipporah, and they had a son. Moses named the boy Gershom, which sounds like the words for "foreigner there." "I have become a foreigner in a foreign land," Moses said.

That name tells you everything about Moses' state of mind. He wasn't home. He wasn't with his people. He was a stranger, tending sheep in a wilderness far from everything he knew.

For forty years. Forty years of silence. Forty years of watching sheep while his people suffered. Forty years of wondering if he'd thrown away his chance to help them.

And what was God doing? Preparing. Moses didn't know it, but every day in that wilderness was training. The patience, the survival skills, the knowledge of the terrain—all of it would be essential when he led Israel through the same wilderness.

God doesn't waste our waiting seasons.

GOD REMEMBERED

Meanwhile, back in Egypt, the suffering continued. "During that long period, the king of Egypt died. The Israelites groaned in their slavery and cried out, and their cry for help went up to God." Four statements about what God did in response:

"God heard their groaning."

WHAT IS THE BOOK OF EXODUS?

"God remembered his covenant with Abraham, with Isaac and with Jacob."

"God looked on the Israelites."

"God was concerned about them."

After centuries of silence, God was about to act. God didn't forget his covenant. When the Bible says God "remembered," it means he's about to act on his promise. He's stepping into the story. The Israelites had cried out in their pain, maybe not even sure he was listening. But he was. And now, finally, the rescue was about to begin.

A shepherd in Midian was about to see a bush on fire.

WHAT THIS MEANS FOR US

First, suffering doesn't mean God has forgotten you. The Israelites suffered for centuries. Generations of them were born, lived, and died as slaves without ever seeing freedom. It would have been easy to think God had abandoned them. But he hadn't. He heard every groan. He saw every tear. And when the time was right, he acted. If you're in a season of suffering right now, don't assume God's silence means God's absence. He may be working in ways you can't see yet.

Second, God's promises outlast every threat against them. Pharaoh threw everything he had at the Israelites—slavery, brutality, genocide. And yet the people kept growing. Why? Because God had promised Abraham that his descendants would become a great nation. No Pharaoh, no matter how powerful, could undo what God had spoken. Whatever threatens you today is not more powerful than God's promises over your life.

Third, ordinary courage matters more than you think.

Shiphrah and Puah weren't queens or prophets. They were midwives—working-class women with no political power. But their decision to fear God more than Pharaoh saved countless lives and helped protect the very nation from which the Messiah would come. You don't have to be powerful to make a difference. You just have to be faithful.

Fourth, God often prepares us in unexpected ways. Moses probably thought his years as a shepherd were wasted time—decades of exile while his people suffered. But God was using that wilderness to train him. The patience, the survival skills, the knowledge of the terrain—all of it would be essential later. Your "wilderness" might be preparation for something you can't imagine yet.

TALKING POINTS

1. **Pharaoh tried to control the Israelite population because he was afraid of losing power.** What are some things people fear losing today that lead them to treat others unjustly? How should trusting God affect our relationship with power?

2. **Shiphrah and Puah had to choose between obeying their king and obeying God.** Have you ever faced a situation where doing the right thing meant going against what everyone else expected? What makes that kind of courage possible?

3. **Moses' mother made the heartbreaking decision to place her baby in a basket on the Nile, trusting God with her son's life.** When have you had to let go of something important and trust God with the outcome? What makes it hard to release control, and what helps us trust that God is taking care of the things and people we love?

4. **Moses' attempt to rescue his people by killing an Egyptian backfired completely.** What's the difference between righteous anger at injustice and taking matters into your own hands in the wrong way? How do we know when to act and when to wait for God?

5. **God was working during the four hundred years of slavery even though it didn't feel like it to the Israelites.** How do you hold onto faith when God seems silent? What helps you trust that he's still at work even when you can't see results?

Moses was an old man now—eighty years old, watching sheep in the middle of nowhere. His dreams of rescuing his people had faded into distant memory. He probably figured his story was over. But God was just getting started. Somewhere in that wilderness, a bush was about to catch fire.

Turn the page.

2

THE BUSH THAT WOULDN'T BURN

In *The Hobbit*, Bilbo Baggins is perfectly happy with his quiet life. He has a comfortable home, regular meals, and no interest in adventures. Then Gandalf the wizard shows up at his door. Gandalf has chosen Bilbo for a dangerous quest—to help dwarves reclaim their homeland from a dragon. Bilbo protests. He's not a hero. He's not brave. He's just a hobbit who likes his armchair. But Gandalf sees something in Bilbo that Bilbo doesn't see in himself.

Exodus 3–4 is the story of God showing up uninvited and choosing the most unlikely person for an impossible mission. Moses is eighty years old, tending sheep in the middle of nowhere, probably assuming his chance to make a difference ended decades ago. Then God appears in a burning bush and says, "I'm sending you to Pharaoh." What follows is one of the longest arguments with God in the entire Bible.

JUST ANOTHER DAY

Moses was doing what he'd done for forty years: watching

sheep. He had led the flock to the far side of the wilderness, near a mountain called Horeb. It was remote, quiet, uneventful—the kind of place where nothing ever happened.

Then something happened.

Moses saw a bush on fire. That wasn't unusual in the desert—dry brush catches fire all the time. But this bush was different. It kept burning without burning up. The flames didn't consume it. Minutes passed, and the bush just kept blazing.

"I will go over and see this strange sight," Moses thought. "Why doesn't the bush burn up?" It was curiosity that drew him closer. He had no idea he was walking toward the most important moment of his life.

HOLY GROUND

When God saw Moses approaching, he called out: "Moses! Moses!"

"Here I am," Moses answered.

"Do not come any closer," God said. "Take off your sandals, for the place where you are standing is holy ground."

The dirt Moses was standing on looked like dirt everywhere else in the wilderness. But God's presence made it different. Where God is, the ordinary becomes sacred.

Then God introduced himself: "I am the God of your father, the God of Abraham, the God of Isaac and the God of Jacob."

Moses hid his face. He was afraid to look at God. For forty years, Moses had been a forgotten exile, a failed rescuer. Now the God of his ancestors—the God who made promises to Abraham centuries ago—was speaking to him directly.

And he had a message.

I HAVE SEEN AND HEARD

"I have indeed seen the misery of my people in Egypt," God said. "I have heard them crying out because of their slave drivers, and I am concerned about their suffering." God hadn't been distant or unaware. He had seen every whip crack, heard every groan. The suffering that seemed invisible to everyone else had been visible to him the entire time. But God wasn't just announcing that he'd been watching. He was about to act.

"So I have come down to rescue them from the hand of the Egyptians and to bring them up out of that land into a good and spacious land, a land flowing with milk and honey." The same land God had promised to Abraham hundreds of years earlier was still the destination. God hadn't forgotten.

But then came the twist. "So now, go. I am sending *you* to Pharaoh to bring my people the Israelites out of Egypt." God was going to rescue his people—through Moses.

EXCUSE #1: WHO AM I?

Moses' first response was probably the most honest thing he'd ever said: "Who am I, that I should go to Pharaoh and bring the Israelites out of Egypt?"

This wasn't false humility. Moses knew exactly who he was. He was a fugitive who had fled Egypt after killing a man. He was a washed up prince who had failed spectacularly the last time he tried to help his people. He was an eighty-year-old shepherd with no army, no influence, and no plan. Pharaoh was the most powerful ruler in the world. Who was Moses to challenge him?

God's answer is one of the most important sentences in the Bible: "I will be with you." Notice what God didn't say.

He didn't say, "You're stronger than you think." He didn't say, "You have untapped potential." He didn't give Moses a pep talk about believing in himself. God said, "I will be with you."

The question wasn't who Moses was. The question was who would be with Moses. And if God was with him, it didn't matter that Moses was old, or scared, or had failed before. God's presence changes everything.

EXCUSE #2: WHO ARE YOU?

Moses had another question: "Suppose I go to the Israelites and say, 'The God of your fathers has sent me,' and they ask, 'What is his name?' Then what shall I tell them?" The Israelites had lived in Egypt for over four hundred years, surrounded by Egyptian gods—dozens of them, each with a name. If Moses showed up claiming to speak for "the God of your fathers," people would naturally ask, "Which god? What's his name?"

God's answer is profound: "I AM WHO I AM. This is what you are to say to the Israelites: 'I AM has sent me to you.'" I AM. This connects to God's personal name—the name written as "the LORD" in English Bibles. It means something like "I am the one who is" or "I will be what I will be."

God isn't like the Egyptian gods, who were tied to specific things—the sun, the Nile, the harvest. God simply *is*. He exists. He's real. He doesn't depend on anything else.

But here's the beautiful part: the first thing God said "I will be" about was his presence with Moses. "I will be with you." God defines himself as the God who is present with his people.

EXCUSE #3: WHAT IF THEY DON'T BELIEVE ME?

"What if they do not believe me or listen to me and say, 'The LORD did not appear to you'?" Moses was about to make an outrageous claim—that God himself had commissioned him to confront Pharaoh. Why should anyone believe him?

So God gave Moses three signs. First, Moses' staff turned into a snake when he threw it on the ground, then back into a staff when he grabbed it. Second, his hand became diseased when he put it in his cloak, then healed when he did it again. Third, God said Moses could pour water from the Nile on the ground and it would turn to blood. These weren't magic tricks. They were credentials—proof that Moses had been sent by the God who made everything.

EXCUSE #4: I CAN'T SPEAK

"O Lord, I have never been eloquent. I am slow of speech and tongue." We don't know exactly what Moses' problem was— maybe a stutter, maybe he struggled under pressure. Whatever it was, Moses felt inadequate for a job requiring a lot of talking.

God's response was firm: "Who gave man his mouth? Who makes him deaf or mute? Who gives him sight or makes him blind? Is it not I, the LORD? Now go; I will help you speak and will teach you what to say." God doesn't call people because they're already qualified. He qualifies the people he calls.

EXCUSE #5: SEND SOMEONE ELSE

Finally, Moses dropped the pretenses: "O Lord, please send someone else to do it." No more reasons. Just a flat refusal.

And for the first time, God got angry.

"What about your brother, Aaron? I know he can speak well. He is already on his way to meet you. You shall speak to him and put words in his mouth. He will speak to the people for you." God gave Moses a partner. Aaron would be Moses' spokesman. It was a concession to Moses' fear—but God didn't let Moses off the hook. He still had to go.

"But take this staff in your hand," God added, "so you can perform miraculous signs with it." The same staff Moses had carried for forty years. This ordinary piece of wood would become the instrument through which God would humble Egypt.

THE ROAD BACK TO EGYPT

Moses returned to Jethro and asked permission to go back to Egypt. Jethro blessed him: "Go in peace." God spoke again: "Go back to Egypt, for all the men who wanted to kill you are dead." Moses took his wife and sons and headed back toward the land he had fled forty years earlier. In his hand was the staff of God.

On the way, something bizarre happened. God met Moses and was about to kill him. Zipporah, Moses' wife, quickly circumcised their son and touched Moses' feet with the blood.

This passage is confusing, but one thing seems clear: Moses had failed to circumcise his son according to Abraham's covenant. Circumcision was the sign of belonging to God's people. If Moses was going to lead Israel, his own household needed to be in order first. Zipporah's quick action saved Moses' life—a jarring reminder that God's mission is serious.

REUNION

Meanwhile, God told Aaron to go into the wilderness to meet Moses. Aaron obeyed, and the brothers reunited at the mountain of God—the same mountain where Moses had seen the burning bush.

Moses told Aaron everything: what God had said, what signs he had given, what mission lay ahead. Then together, they traveled to Egypt.

When they arrived, they gathered the elders of Israel. Aaron spoke all the words God had given Moses, and Moses performed the signs in front of the people.

And the Israelites believed. After four hundred years of slavery, after generations of crying out, after decades of silence—they believed that God had seen them, heard them, and was finally coming to rescue them. They bowed down and worshiped.

WHAT THIS MEANS FOR US

First, God often calls unlikely people. Moses was old, scared, and had a history of failure. He had every reason to think his chance had passed. But God doesn't choose people based on their résumés. He chooses people and then equips them for what he's called them to do. If you feel unqualified for what God is asking of you, you're in good company.

Second, God's presence matters more than your ability. Every objection Moses raised was about himself—his weakness, his inadequacy, his limitations. God's answer was always the same: "I will be with you." The most important thing about any mission isn't who you are. It's who is with you.

Third, excuses eventually run out. Moses had legitimate concerns, and God addressed them patiently. But when Moses simply said, "Send someone else," God got angry. There's a difference between honest questions and stubborn refusal. God welcomes our doubts. He doesn't welcome our disobedience.

Fourth, God uses ordinary tools for extraordinary purposes. Moses' staff was just a stick—something he'd carried every day for forty years. But in God's hands, it became an instrument of miracles. God loves to take the ordinary things in our lives and use them for his glory.

TALKING POINTS

1. **Moses gave five different excuses for why he couldn't do what God asked.** Which of his objections do you relate to most? Why do you think it's so hard to trust God when he calls us to do something difficult?

2. **God's answer to Moses' fear was "I will be with you."** Why is God's presence more important than our own abilities? How does knowing God is with you change the way you face scary situations?

3. **God revealed his name to Moses as "I AM WHO I AM."** Why do you think names are so important in the Bible? What does it mean for your life that God is the same yesterday, today, and forever—that he's the same God who spoke to Moses and who is with you now?

4. **Moses' staff was an ordinary shepherd's tool that became an instrument of miracles.** What ordinary things in your life might God want to use for his purposes? How can we be open to God using the everyday parts of our lives?

5. **The Israelites had been waiting for rescue for over four hundred years.** When Moses and Aaron finally arrived with God's message, they believed and worshiped. What does their response teach us about how to react when God finally answers prayers we've been praying for a long time?

The shepherd was heading back to Egypt. The staff was in his hand. The God who had been silent for four hundred years had spoken. Now came the hard part. Moses had to face Pharaoh—and Pharaoh wasn't going to listen.

Turn the page.

3

THINGS GET WORSE BEFORE THEY GET BETTER

Have you ever tried to help someone and ended up making things worse? In the movie *Lilo & Stitch*, Stitch is an alien experiment designed for destruction. When he crash-lands on Earth and gets adopted by a lonely girl named Lilo, he tries to become part of her family. But every time he attempts to help—making dinner, doing chores, anything—chaos erupts. Things break. People get hurt. Lilo's older sister Nani nearly loses custody of Lilo because of the disasters Stitch causes. For a while, it looks like Stitch's presence has made everything worse, not better.

That's exactly what happens when Moses goes to Pharaoh. God had promised to rescue his people. Moses and Aaron marched into the palace, delivered God's message, and expected things to start improving. Instead, everything fell apart. The Israelites' suffering doubled. Their own leaders blamed Moses. And Moses was left wondering if God had made a terrible mistake.

Welcome to Exodus 5. Sometimes, following God makes things worse before they get better.

LET MY PEOPLE GO

Moses and Aaron walked into Pharaoh's throne room with the most powerful message in the world: "This is what the LORD, the God of Israel, says: 'Let my people go, so that they may hold a festival to me in the wilderness.'" This wasn't a polite request. It was a command from the Creator of the universe. Moses and Aaron were ambassadors—God's official representatives, speaking with his authority. What they said, God said.

Pharaoh's response tells you everything you need to know about him: "Who is the LORD, that I should obey him and let Israel go? I do not know the LORD and I will not let Israel go."

Who is the LORD? Pharaoh wasn't just asking for information. He was dismissing Israel's God as unimportant. Egypt had dozens of gods—gods of the sun, the Nile, the harvest, the dead. Pharaoh himself was considered divine. Why should the most powerful ruler in the world care about some god worshiped by his slaves?

"I do not know the LORD," Pharaoh declared. "I will not let Israel go." By the end of Exodus, Pharaoh will know exactly who the Lord is. But it will take ten devastating plagues to teach him.

MAKE THEIR WORK HARDER

Moses and Aaron tried again: "The God of the Hebrews has met with us. Please let us take a three-day journey into the wilderness to offer sacrifices to the LORD our God." Pharaoh wasn't interested. "Why are you taking the people away from their labor? Get back to your work!"

But Pharaoh didn't stop there. He decided to punish the Israelites for even asking. "You are no longer to supply the people with straw for making bricks," he ordered his slave drivers. "Let them go and gather their own straw. But require them to make the same number of bricks as before; don't reduce the quota. They are lazy; that is why they are crying out, 'Let us go and sacrifice to our God.' Make the work harder for the people so that they keep working and pay no attention to lies."

This was cruel beyond measure. Making bricks required straw—it was mixed with clay to hold the bricks together. Until now, the Egyptians had provided straw for the Israelites. Now the slaves had to scatter across the country, gathering stubble from the fields, while still meeting their impossible quotas.

The slave drivers beat the Israelite foremen when the quotas weren't met. The foremen appealed directly to Pharaoh, but he refused to listen. "Lazy, that's what you are—lazy!" he mocked. "Now get to work." Moses had asked for freedom. The result was more suffering.

BLAME MOSES

When the Israelite foremen left Pharaoh's palace, they ran into Moses and Aaron waiting outside. Their words were brutal: "May the LORD look on you and judge you! You have made us obnoxious to Pharaoh and his officials and have put a sword in their hand to kill us."

Put yourself in Moses' sandals. He had finally obeyed God. He had overcome his fears, returned to Egypt, confronted the most powerful ruler on earth. And now his own people were cursing him. The very people he was trying to save wanted God to punish him. Moses had expected resistance from Pharaoh. He hadn't expected his own people to turn against him.

This is what happens when things get worse before they get better. People look for someone to blame. And the easiest target is often the person trying to help.

WHY, LORD?

Moses did the only thing he could do. He went back to God. "Why, Lord, why have you brought trouble on this people? Is this why you sent me? Ever since I went to Pharaoh to speak in your name, he has brought trouble on this people, and you have not rescued your people at all."

This is one of the most honest prayers in the Bible. Moses isn't pretending everything is fine. He's not putting on a spiritual mask. He's confused, frustrated, and maybe a little angry. He's asking God the question that believers have asked for thousands of years: *Why is this happening? You promised to help, but things are getting worse!*

Notice something important: Moses didn't walk away from God. He walked *toward* God. When everything fell apart, he didn't abandon his mission or give up on God's promises. He brought his confusion straight to the source.

That's what faith looks like when things go wrong. Not pretending you don't have doubts. Not acting like everything is fine when it isn't. But taking your questions—even your hardest, most painful questions—directly to God.

NOW YOU WILL SEE

God's answer didn't explain everything. He didn't give Moses a detailed timeline or apologize for the delay. But he did give Moses something better: a promise.

"Now you will see what I will do to Pharaoh: Because of my mighty hand he will let them go; because of my mighty hand he will drive them out of his country." God was still in control. The disaster at the palace wasn't a sign that God's plan had failed. It was setting the stage for something bigger.

Think about it. If Pharaoh had agreed to Moses' first request, the Israelites would have gone on a three-day trip and come back. The Egyptians would have said, "Sure, take a holiday. No big deal." There would have been no dramatic rescue, no display of God's power, no lesson for the nations about who the Lord really is.

But now? Pharaoh had publicly defied God. He had increased the oppression. He had drawn a line in the sand. And God was about to show exactly what happens when a human ruler challenges the Creator of the universe. "Now you will see."

I AM THE LORD

God spoke to Moses again, and this time he went deeper. He reminded Moses of who he was and what he had promised. "I am the LORD. I appeared to Abraham, to Isaac and to Jacob as God Almighty, but by my name the LORD I did not make myself fully known to them."

The patriarchs—Abraham, Isaac, Jacob—had known God. They had received his promises. But they had never seen God act on the scale that Moses was about to witness. They knew God as the one who *makes* promises. Moses would know God as the one who *keeps* them.

Then came the seven "I wills"—seven promises that laid out exactly what God was about to do:

"I will bring you out from under the yoke of the Egyptians."

"I will free you from being slaves to them."

"I will redeem you with an outstretched arm and with mighty acts of judgment."

"I will take you as my own people."

"I will be your God."

"I will bring you to the land I swore with uplifted hand to give to Abraham, to Isaac and to Jacob."

"I will give it to you as a possession."

Seven promises. Absolute certainty. God wasn't asking Pharaoh's permission. He was announcing what he was going to do.

THEY DID NOT LISTEN

Moses reported all this to the Israelites. But they didn't want to hear it. "They did not listen to him because of their discouragement and harsh labor."

Can you blame them? Their backs were raw from beatings. Their quotas had doubled. The last time they believed Moses, everything got worse. Why should they trust him now?

This is one of the saddest verses in Exodus. God had just made the most incredible promises—freedom, redemption, a homeland, a relationship with him. And his people were too beaten down to receive them.

Suffering can do that. When you've been hurt enough times, hope starts to feel dangerous. It's easier not to believe than to be disappointed again.

But here's the thing: their unbelief didn't change God's plan. God would rescue them whether they felt hopeful or not. His promises don't depend on our emotional state.

BACK TO PHARAOH

God sent Moses back to Pharaoh. Moses protested—if even the Israelites wouldn't listen to him, why would Pharaoh?

But God didn't debate with Moses. He simply gave him his orders. Moses and Aaron would go to Pharaoh. Aaron would speak. And God would harden Pharaoh's heart.

Wait—God would harden Pharaoh's heart? What does that mean?

This is one of the most debated questions in the whole book of Exodus. Sometimes the text says Pharaoh hardened his own heart. Other times it says God hardened Pharaoh's heart. How do we understand this?

Think of it this way: Pharaoh had already decided who he was. He had already declared, "I do not know the LORD and I will not let Israel go." He had already chosen defiance. God didn't force Pharaoh to be someone he wasn't. He simply strengthened Pharaoh in the direction Pharaoh had already chosen.

And God did this for a purpose: "I will harden Pharaoh's heart, and though I multiply my signs and wonders in Egypt, he will not listen to you. Then I will lay my hand on Egypt and with mighty acts of judgment I will bring out my people." God was going to use Pharaoh's stubbornness to display his power. Every time Pharaoh refused, another plague would come. And with every plague, Egypt and the watching world—would learn who the Lord really is. "The Egyptians will know that I am the LORD when I stretch out my hand against Egypt and bring the Israelites out of it."

SNAKES AND STAFFS

Moses and Aaron went back to Pharaoh. When Pharaoh demanded a miracle, Aaron threw down his staff. It became a snake.

But Pharaoh wasn't impressed. He summoned his own magicians, and they did the same thing—their staffs became snakes too.

This could have been discouraging. If Egypt's magicians could match God's power, what was the point?

But then something happened that the magicians couldn't duplicate: Aaron's snake swallowed all of their snakes.

It was a small detail, but it carried a massive message. Egypt's magic was real, but it was nothing compared to the Lord's power. The God of Israel didn't just match the Egyptian gods. He devoured them.

Still, Pharaoh's heart was hard. He refused to listen.

The plagues were about to begin.

WHAT THIS MEANS FOR US

First, obedience doesn't always produce immediate results. Moses obeyed God completely, and the immediate result was disaster. The Israelites' suffering increased. His own people blamed him. If you're doing the right thing and everything seems to be going wrong, you're in good company. Sometimes things get worse before they get better.

Second, it's okay to bring your questions to God. Moses didn't pretend to be fine. He asked God hard questions—"Why, Lord?" That's not a lack of faith. That's real faith, the kind that wrestles with God instead of walking away from him. God can handle your doubts.

Third, God's plan doesn't depend on our feelings. The Israelites were too discouraged to believe God's promises. But God kept his promises anyway. Your emotional state doesn't determine God's faithfulness. Even when you can't feel hope, his word is still true.

Fourth, God's power always wins. The Egyptian magicians could do impressive tricks, but Aaron's snake swallowed theirs. No matter how powerful the opposition looks, God's power is greater. The contest between the Lord and Pharaoh was never a fair fight—because no one can stand against the Creator of the universe.

TALKING POINTS

1. **When Moses obeyed God, things got worse before they got better.** Have you ever experienced a situation where doing the right thing seemed to make things harder? How did you respond?

2. **Moses brought his frustration and questions directly to God instead of walking away.** Why do you think it's important to be honest with God about our doubts and struggles instead of pretending everything is fine?

3. **The Israelites were too discouraged to believe God's promises.** What makes it hard to hold onto hope when we're going through difficult times? What helps you trust God even when you don't feel hopeful?

4. **God said the Egyptians would "know that I am the LORD" through the plagues.** What does it mean to truly *know* God, not just know *about* him? How is knowing God personally different from just believing he exists?

5. **Pharaoh's magicians could imitate some of what God did, but their power was limited.** How do you tell the difference between what's truly from God and what's a counterfeit? Why do you think God allowed the magicians to copy some miracles before showing his greater power?

The contest had begun. Pharaoh had drawn the line. He had declared that he didn't know the Lord and wouldn't let Israel go. He was about to find out exactly who the Lord is. The Nile was about to turn to blood.

Turn the page.

4

THE GOD WHO FIGHTS BACK

In *Avatar: The Last Airbender*, the Fire Nation has conquered nearly everything. Their armies are unstoppable. Their technology is unmatched. For a hundred years, they've crushed every nation that stood against them—the Air Nomads are gone, the Water Tribes are barely surviving, and the Earth Kingdom is slowly falling. The Fire Lord sits on his throne, believing no one can challenge him.

Then a young boy is freed from being frozen in an iceberg. Aang, the Avatar, doesn't look like much of a threat. He's young, untrained, and has been missing for a century. But he has something the Fire Nation can't defeat: the power to control all four elements. Over the course of the series, Aang and his friends chip away at the Fire Nation's confidence. Battle by battle, victory by victory, they prove that the Fire Lord's power has limits—that there's a force in the world stronger than fire.

That's what the plagues of Egypt were like. Pharaoh sat on his throne, surrounded by his gods and his magicians, convinced that no one could challenge him. Then God started fighting back. Blow by blow, plague by plague, God systematically dismantled everything Egypt trusted in. By the time it was over, Pharaoh would know exactly who the Lord was—even if it destroyed him to learn it.

NOT JUST PUNISHMENTS—A BATTLE

Before we walk through the plagues, you need to understand what they actually were. These weren't random disasters. They weren't just punishments for Pharaoh's stubbornness. They were targeted strikes against the gods of Egypt.

Egypt had dozens of gods—gods of the Nile, gods of the land, gods of the sky. The Egyptians believed these gods controlled everything: the flooding of the river, the fertility of their crops, the rising of the sun. Pharaoh himself was considered divine—a god in human form, responsible for maintaining order in the universe. When Pharaoh asked, "Who is the LORD that I should obey him?" he wasn't just being arrogant. He genuinely believed he was a god and that his gods were more powerful than any foreign deity.

When God sent the plagues, he was sending a message: "Your gods are nothing. I am the LORD, and there is no other." Each plague attacked something the Egyptians worshiped. The Nile turned to blood? The Egyptians worshiped the Nile as a god named Hapi. Frogs overran the land? The Egyptians had a frog goddess named Heqet. Darkness covered Egypt? The Egyptians worshiped Ra, the sun god, as the most powerful deity of all. Plague after plague, God was proving that the gods of Egypt were powerless to protect their people.

Later, God would describe what he did in Egypt this way: "I will bring judgment on all the gods of Egypt. I am the LORD."

This was a theological battle, not just a political one. And God was winning.

PLAGUE 1: BLOOD

God told Moses to meet Pharaoh at the Nile in the morning. When Pharaoh arrived—perhaps for his daily ritual honoring the river gods—Moses delivered God's message: "By this you will know that I am the LORD." Then Aaron raised his staff and struck the water. The entire Nile turned to blood. Every stream, every canal, every pond in Egypt—blood. The fish died. The river stank. The Egyptians couldn't drink from it.

The Nile was Egypt's lifeblood. It provided water, food, transportation—everything. And God turned it into death. But Pharaoh's magicians did the same thing with their secret arts. They turned some water into blood too. (Where they found water that wasn't already blood, the text doesn't say.) Pharaoh saw his magicians match the miracle and walked back into his palace, unimpressed.

His heart remained hard.

PLAGUE 2: FROGS

Seven days later, God struck again. This time: frogs. Not just some frogs—frogs *everywhere*. They came up from the Nile and invaded everything. Into homes. Into bedrooms. Into beds. Into ovens. Into bread bowls. Frogs covering the ground, frogs in your food, frogs in your face.

Again, the magicians replicated the plague. They made more frogs appear. (Thanks a lot, guys. More frogs is exactly what Egypt needed.)

But this time, Pharaoh cracked. He summoned Moses and Aaron and said, "Pray to the LORD to take the frogs away from me and my people, and I will let your people go."

Moses agreed—and gave Pharaoh an unusual choice. "I leave to you the honor of setting the time for me to pray."

"Tomorrow," Pharaoh said.

Think about that. Pharaoh was so miserable he begged for relief—then asked to wait until *tomorrow*? One more night with frogs in his bed? It's almost funny. But Moses agreed, specifically so Pharaoh would know "there is no one like the LORD our God."

God answered Moses' prayer. The frogs died—in the houses, in the courtyards, in the fields. The Egyptians piled them into heaps, and the whole land reeked. But when Pharaoh saw the relief, he hardened his heart. He didn't let the people go.

PLAGUE 3: GNATS

This time there was no warning. God simply told Moses to have Aaron strike the dust of the ground. When he did, the dust became gnats—tiny biting insects that covered people and animals throughout Egypt.

The magicians tried to replicate this plague. They couldn't. "This is the finger of God," they told Pharaoh. Even Pharaoh's own magicians admitted they were outmatched. But Pharaoh's heart remained hard.

PLAGUE 4: FLIES

With the fourth plague, something new happened. God announced that he would make a distinction between Egypt and

Goshen, where the Israelites lived. The flies would swarm over Egypt, but not a single fly would touch Goshen. "I will deal differently with the land of Goshen, where my people live," God said. "I will make a distinction between my people and your people."

This was crucial. Pharaoh couldn't dismiss the plagues as natural disasters that affected everyone equally. The Israelites were protected. God was specifically targeting Egypt while sparing his own people.

The flies came—dense swarms that ruined the land. Pharaoh summoned Moses again and offered a compromise: "Go, sacrifice to your God here in the land."

Moses refused. Egyptian worship practices would be offensive to them, he explained. They needed to go three days into the wilderness.

Pharaoh relented slightly: "I will let you go to offer sacrifices to the LORD your God in the wilderness, but you must not go very far."

Moses agreed to pray. God removed the flies. And Pharaoh hardened his heart and refused to let the people go.

PLAGUE 5: LIVESTOCK

The fifth plague struck Egypt's animals—horses, donkeys, camels, cattle, sheep, and goats. A terrible disease killed them in the fields.

Again, God made a distinction. Not one animal belonging to the Israelites died. Pharaoh even sent officials to check— and confirmed that Israel's livestock was untouched.

It didn't matter. Pharaoh's heart remained hard.

PLAGUE 6: BOILS

For the sixth plague, Moses and Aaron threw handfuls of furnace soot into the air. It became fine dust that spread over all of Egypt, and wherever it landed, painful boils broke out on people and animals.

The magicians who had been trying to match God's power? They couldn't even stand before Moses because of the boils covering their bodies. They were done. From this point on, they disappear from the story.

But the Lord hardened Pharaoh's heart, and he refused to listen—just as God had told Moses would happen.

PLAGUE 7: HAIL

The seventh plague came with a warning—and an opportunity. God told Moses to announce to Pharaoh that the worst hailstorm in Egypt's history was coming. But God also gave the Egyptians a chance to protect themselves: "Give an order now to bring your livestock and everything you have in the field to a place of shelter, because the hail will fall on every person and animal that has not been brought in."

Some Egyptian officials believed the warning and brought their servants and animals inside. Others ignored it and left everything in the fields.

Then the hail came—mixed with fire, the worst storm Egypt had ever seen. It killed everything left outside: people, animals, crops. Only in Goshen, where the Israelites lived, was there no hail.

Pharaoh summoned Moses and made a remarkable confession: "This time I have sinned. The LORD is in the right, and I and my people are in the wrong."

Moses agreed to pray. But he also said something piercing: "I know that you and your officials still do not fear the LORD God." He was right. As soon as the storm stopped, Pharaoh hardened his heart again.

PLAGUE 8: LOCUSTS

Before the eighth plague, even Pharaoh's own officials turned against him. "How long will this man be a snare to us?" they demanded. "Let the people go! Do you not yet realize that Egypt is ruined?"

Pharaoh brought Moses and Aaron back and asked who exactly would be going to worship the Lord. "Everyone," Moses answered. "Young and old, sons and daughters, flocks and herds." Pharaoh refused. He would let only the men go.

So God sent locusts—driven by an east wind that blew all day and all night. By morning, the locusts had invaded. They covered the ground until it was black. They devoured everything the hail had left: every plant, every tree. Nothing green remained.

Pharaoh summoned Moses in a panic. "I have sinned against the LORD your God and against you. Now forgive my sin once more and pray to the LORD your God to take this deadly plague away from me."

Moses prayed. God sent a powerful west wind that swept every locust into the Red Sea. Not a single locust remained. But the Lord hardened Pharaoh's heart, and he would not let the Israelites go.

PLAGUE 9: DARKNESS

The ninth plague was different. No warning. No negotiation. Just sudden, total darkness. Moses stretched out his hand toward the sky, and a darkness fell over Egypt—thick darkness that could be felt. For three days, the Egyptians couldn't see each other. They couldn't move from where they were. They sat paralyzed in a darkness so complete it was like being blind.

But all the Israelites had light where they lived.

Think about what this meant. The Egyptians worshiped Ra, the sun god, more than almost any other deity. Ra was supposed to be the source of all light and life. Every morning when the sun rose, Egyptians believed Ra had defeated the forces of chaos once again. The sun's daily journey across the sky was proof of Ra's power.

And for three days, Ra was utterly powerless. The sun god couldn't make the sun shine. The most powerful god in Egypt's pantheon had been silenced, shut down, defeated without a fight.

Pharaoh called for Moses. "Go, worship the LORD," he said. "Even your women and children may go with you; only leave your flocks and herds behind." It was another compromise. Another attempt to negotiate. Another refusal to fully obey. Moses refused. "Not a hoof is to be left behind." The Lord hardened Pharaoh's heart, and he was unwilling to let them go.

GET OUT OF MY SIGHT

What happened next was a complete breakdown. Pharaoh was done negotiating. He was done seeing Moses' face. In a rage, he issued a death threat: "Get out of my sight! Make sure you do not appear before me again! The day you see my face you will die."

Moses' response was calm but loaded with meaning: "Just as you say. I will never appear before you again." Pharaoh thought he was dismissing Moses. He thought he was ending the conversation on his terms. But Moses knew something Pharaoh didn't: this was Pharaoh's last chance. One more plague was coming—the worst of all—and after that, Pharaoh wouldn't be making demands anymore.

THE PATTERN

Looking back over these nine plagues, several patterns emerge.

First, notice the escalation. The plagues started as annoyances (bloody water, frogs) and grew into catastrophes (livestock death, hail, locusts, darkness). God gave Pharaoh every opportunity to repent before things got worse.

Second, notice Pharaoh's cycle. Over and over, when the pressure was on, Pharaoh begged for relief and promised to let the people go. But the moment the plague was removed, he went back on his word. His confessions of sin were never sincere. He never truly feared the Lord.

Third, notice the growing distinction between Egypt and Israel. Starting with the fourth plague, God made it clear that his people were protected. The plagues weren't random—they were targeted. And Pharaoh could see with his own eyes that Israel's God was real and powerful.

Fourth, notice who hardened Pharaoh's heart. Sometimes the text says Pharaoh hardened his own heart. Other times it says God hardened Pharaoh's heart. Both are true. Pharaoh chose stubbornness from the beginning. God used that stubbornness to display his power to the nations.

WHAT THIS MEANS FOR US

First, there is no god like the Lord. The plagues systematically dismantled every false god Egypt trusted in. Whatever you're tempted to put your trust in—money, popularity, your own abilities—none of it can stand against the living God. He alone is worthy of worship.

Second, God is patient but not passive. Nine plagues. Nine chances for Pharaoh to repent. God warned, waited, and warned again. But his patience had a limit. Eventually, judgment came. The same God who patiently calls people to turn to him is also the God who will hold people accountable for their choices.

Third, partial obedience is still disobedience. Pharaoh kept trying to negotiate—letting only the men go, keeping the livestock behind. Every compromise was a refusal to fully obey. God doesn't accept half-hearted obedience. He wants all of us, not just the parts we're comfortable giving.

Fourth, God protects his people. The distinction between Egypt and Goshen is one of the most beautiful pictures in this story. While judgment fell on Egypt, God's people had light. While Egypt suffered, Israel was safe. Those who belong to God can trust that he sees them, knows them, and will protect them.

TALKING POINTS

1. **Each plague attacked something the Egyptians worshiped.** What are some things people today put their trust in instead of God? How might God show that those things can't ultimately save us?

2. **Pharaoh repeatedly promised to obey God when he was suffering, then went back on his word when the pressure was removed.** Why do you think people sometimes act more religious during hard times but forget God when things get easier?

3. **God made a clear distinction between Egypt and Goshen—his people were protected while Egypt suffered.** How does knowing that God protects and cares for his people affect the way you think about difficult situations in the world?

4. **Pharaoh kept trying to compromise—letting only some people go or keeping the livestock behind.** Why do you think God rejected these partial offers? What does this teach us about what God expects from us?

5. **The plague of darkness was so thick it could be "felt."** What does light and darkness symbolize in the Bible? How does being in relationship with God bring "light" to our lives in ways that go beyond physical sight?

Nine plagues had fallen. The Nile had turned to blood. Frogs, gnats, and flies had swarmed the land. Livestock had died. Boils had covered the Egyptians. Hail had destroyed the crops. Locusts had devoured what remained. Darkness had smothered the land for three days. And still Pharaoh refused.

One plague remained—the most terrible of all. The one God had promised from the very beginning: "Israel is my firstborn son. Let my son go, so he may worship me. If you refuse, I will kill your firstborn son."

Pharaoh had refused. Now the angel of death was coming. Turn the page.

5

BLOOD ON THE DOORFRAME

In *The Lord of the Rings*, there's a moment when everything hangs in the balance. Frodo stands at the edge of Mount Doom, the fires roaring below, the Ring finally within reach of destruction. For three books (or three very long movies), the entire story has been building to this moment. The fate of Middle-earth depends on what happens next. All the battles, all the journeys, all the sacrifices—they've all been leading here.

The Passover is that moment in the story of Exodus. For nine plagues, God had been dismantling Egypt piece by piece. Pharaoh had been warned, given chances, shown mercy. But his heart remained hard. Now the final blow was coming—the one God had promised from the very beginning, back when he first spoke to Moses at the burning bush: "Israel is my firstborn son. Let my son go, so he may worship me. If you refuse, I will kill your firstborn son." Pharaoh had refused. Now death was coming to Egypt.

But this chapter isn't just about judgment on Egypt. It's about salvation for Israel. And the way God saved his people that night would echo through the rest of Scripture, all the way to Jesus himself.

THE ANNOUNCEMENT

Moses delivered God's final message to Pharaoh: "About midnight I will go throughout Egypt. Every firstborn son in Egypt will die, from the firstborn son of Pharaoh, who sits on the throne, to the firstborn son of the slave girl, who is at her hand mill, and all the firstborn of the cattle as well."

No one would escape. From the palace to the poorest hovel, from the throne room to the grinding mill, death would visit every Egyptian household. The wailing would be worse than anything Egypt had ever experienced—or ever would again.

But among the Israelites? "Not a dog will bark at any person or animal." God would make a distinction. He would separate his people from their oppressors. The same night that brought death to Egypt would bring deliverance to Israel.

After delivering this message, Moses left Pharaoh's presence, burning with anger. He would never stand before Pharaoh again.

THE LAMB

But here's the part that might surprise you: the Israelites weren't automatically safe. They weren't protected just because they were Israelites. They had to do something. They had to trust God and obey his instructions.

God gave Moses detailed instructions for what would become the most important night in Israel's history—and the most important ritual in their calendar. On the tenth day of the month, each family was to select a lamb—a year-old male without any defects. They were to care for it until the fourteenth day. Then, at twilight, they were to slaughter it.

But the blood wasn't wasted. God told them to take hyssop branches, dip them in the blood, and paint it on the tops and sides of their doorframes. Then they were to stay inside their houses until morning. "When I see the blood," God said, "I will pass over you. No destructive plague will touch you when I strike Egypt." This is where the word "Passover" comes from. God would pass over the houses marked with blood. Death would pass over those homes and move on.

Think about what this meant. The lamb died so the first-born could live. The blood of an innocent animal was the difference between life and death. It wasn't the nationality of the family that saved them—it was the blood on the doorframe.

THE MEAL

The Israelites weren't just supposed to kill the lamb. They were supposed to eat it. God gave specific instructions: roast the meat over fire (don't boil it), eat it with bitter herbs and bread made without yeast, and don't leave any of it until morning. Whatever was left over had to be burned.

And here's the strange part: they were supposed to eat it dressed for travel. Cloak tucked into their belt. Sandals on their feet. Staff in hand. Ready to go. They were eating a meal as if they were about to run out the door—because they were. God was telling them, "This is really happening. Tonight, you're leaving Egypt. Be ready."

The bitter herbs reminded them of the bitterness of slavery. The bread without yeast (unleavened bread) reminded them of how quickly they would have to leave—no time to let bread rise. Every element of the meal told a story.

WHAT IS THE BOOK OF EXODUS?

THE NIGHT OF DEATH

At midnight, the Lord struck down all the firstborn in Egypt. The text is simple and devastating: "From the firstborn of Pharaoh, who sat on the throne, to the firstborn of the prisoner, who was in the dungeon, and the firstborn of all the livestock as well."

Pharaoh woke in the night. His officials woke. All of Egypt woke. And in every home where the blood was not on the doorframe, someone was dead. "There was loud wailing in Egypt, for there was not a house without someone dead."

The prince of Egypt—heir to the throne, future god-king in Egyptian belief—was gone. The sons of officials and soldiers and merchants and farmers and prisoners—gone. The grief was universal, inescapable, unbearable.

Pharaoh had tried to kill Israel's sons. Now his own son was dead. This was justice. Terrible, devastating justice. The Egyptians had enslaved God's people for generations. They had thrown Hebrew babies into the Nile. They had worked the Israelites to death. And now the God of Israel had proven that he was Lord of life and death—and that he would not let his people be destroyed.

GET OUT

That same night, Pharaoh summoned Moses and Aaron. "Up! Leave my people, you and the Israelites! Go, worship the LORD as you have requested. Take your flocks and herds, as you have said, and go. And also bless me."

No more negotiations. No more conditions. No more compromises. Just: *Get out.* The Egyptians urged the Israelites to hurry. "We will all be dead!" they said. They even gave the Israelites silver and gold and clothing—whatever they asked for. After everything that had happened, the Egyptians just wanted them gone.

So the Israelites left. Six hundred thousand men on foot, plus women and children—a massive multitude, along with their livestock and their dough (still without yeast, because there was no time to let it rise). A "mixed multitude" went with them too—non-Israelites who had seen what God had done and decided to throw their lot in with his people.

After 430 years in Egypt, the Israelites walked out as free people.

REMEMBER THIS DAY

God told Moses that the Israelites were to remember this night forever. Every year, on the anniversary of their deliverance, they were to celebrate the Passover. They were to tell their children the story. When their kids asked, "What does this ceremony mean?" the parents were to answer: "It is the Passover sacrifice to the LORD, who passed over the houses of the Israelites in Egypt and spared our homes when he struck down the Egyptians."

The Passover wasn't just a memorial. It was an identity. It told Israel who they were: a people saved by the blood of a lamb, delivered from slavery by the mighty hand of God.

And here's what's remarkable: the Passover would be celebrated for over a thousand years—and then, on a Passover night in Jerusalem, Jesus would share one final Passover meal with his disciples before going to the cross. The Lamb of God would become the sacrifice that would save people not just from slavery in Egypt but from slavery to sin and death itself.

TRAPPED

But the story wasn't over yet. Pharaoh let the Israelites go. But as they traveled toward the wilderness, his heart changed again. "What have we done? We have let the Israelites go and have lost their services!" He gathered his army—six hundred of his best chariots, plus all the other chariots of Egypt—and chased after them.

The Israelites had camped by the sea. When they looked up and saw the Egyptian army thundering toward them, they were terrified. They were trapped. The sea was in front of them. The desert was on either side. The most powerful army in the world was behind them. There was nowhere to go.

"Was it because there were no graves in Egypt that you brought us to the desert to die?" they cried to Moses. "What have you done to us by bringing us out of Egypt? Didn't we say to you in Egypt, 'Leave us alone; let us serve the Egyptians'? It would have been better for us to serve the Egyptians than to die in the desert!" It's easy to criticize their fear. But put yourself in their position. No weapons. No military training. Women and children and elderly and livestock. And Pharaoh's chariots bearing down on them at full speed.

STAND FIRM

Moses' response was one of the greatest statements of faith in the entire Bible: "Do not be afraid. Stand firm and you will see the deliverance the LORD will bring you today. The Egyptians you see today you will never see again. The LORD will fight for you; you need only to be still." Don't be afraid. Stand firm. Watch what God is about to do.

Then God told Moses to raise his staff over the sea.

THE SEA PARTS

Moses stretched out his hand over the sea, and all that night the Lord drove the sea back with a strong east wind. The waters divided, and the Israelites walked through the sea on dry ground, with a wall of water on their right and on their left.

Think about that. Walls of water towering on both sides. The wind howling. The ground beneath their feet—dry ground in the middle of the sea. Thousands upon thousands of people walking through, carrying children, leading animals, watching the impossible happen right before their eyes.

Meanwhile, the pillar of cloud that had been leading them moved behind them, standing between Israel and the Egyptian army all night long. It brought darkness to the Egyptian side but light to the Israelite side. Pharaoh's army couldn't advance until morning.

THE SEA CLOSES

At dawn, the Egyptians pursued. Chariots and horses and soldiers charged into the seabed after the Israelites. But God threw them into confusion. Wheels came off chariots. Horses stumbled. The Egyptians realized too late what was happening: "Let's get away from the Israelites! The LORD is fighting for them against Egypt!"

Then God told Moses to stretch out his hand over the sea again. Moses obeyed. And the sea flowed back. The water swept over the chariots and horsemen—the entire army of Pharaoh that had followed the Israelites into the sea. Not one of them survived.

The Israelites stood on the far shore and watched. Egyptian bodies washed up on the sand. The most powerful army in the world—destroyed in a moment by the God who controls the waters. "And when the Israelites saw the mighty hand of the LORD displayed against the Egyptians, the people feared the LORD and put their trust in him and in Moses his servant."

THE SONG

What do you do after something like that?

You sing.

Moses and the Israelites sang a song to the Lord—one of the oldest and most beautiful poems in the Bible: "I will sing to the LORD, for he is highly exalted. Both horse and driver he has hurled into the sea. The LORD is my strength and my defense; he has become my salvation. He is my God, and I will praise him, my father's God, and I will exalt him."

The song celebrated who God is: a warrior, majestic in power, unmatched by any so-called god. It recounted what God had done: blowing away the enemy with his breath, sinking them like stones, swallowing them in the depths. It marveled at God's character: "Who among the gods is like you, LORD? Who is like you—majestic in holiness, awesome in glory, working wonders?"

And it looked forward to what God would do: lead his people, plant them in the land he promised, dwell among them forever.

"The LORD reigns for ever and ever."

Miriam, Moses' sister—called a prophetess, one of the leaders of Israel alongside her brothers—took a tambourine and led the women in dancing and singing. "Sing to the LORD, for he is highly exalted. Both horse and driver he has hurled into the sea."

This wasn't polite worship. This was wild celebration. Dancing and drums and shouting and joy. These were former slaves who had just watched their oppressors destroyed. They were alive when they should have been recaptured or killed. They were free when they should have been back in chains. How could they not sing?

WHAT THIS MEANS FOR US

First, salvation comes through blood. The Passover lamb died so that Israel's firstborn could live. This points forward to Jesus, "the Lamb of God who takes away the sin of the world." Just as the lamb's blood marked the Israelites' doorframes and protected them from death, Jesus's blood covers our sins and protects us from judgment.

Second, God fights for his people. The Israelites didn't defeat the Egyptian army. God did. "The LORD will fight for you; you need only to be still." When we face impossible situations, we can trust that the God who parted the sea is still fighting for us.

Third, our God is incomparable. "Who among the gods is like you, LORD?" the song asks. The answer is: no one. The gods of Egypt were exposed as powerless. There is no god like the God of Israel—no one as majestic, as holy, as powerful, as worthy of praise.

Fourth, God's salvation calls for a response. The Israelites didn't just walk away from the Red Sea in silence. They sang.

They danced. They worshiped. When we experience God's salvation, praise should be our instinctive response.

TALKING POINTS

1. **The lamb's blood on the doorframe was the difference between life and death.** How does this help you understand what Jesus's death on the cross means for you?

2. **The Israelites had to eat the Passover meal dressed and ready to leave.** Why do you think God wanted them to be ready to move immediately? What does it look like in your own life to be ready and expectant for God to act, rather than getting too comfortable where you are?

3. **When the Israelites saw Pharaoh's army, they panicked and complained.** Moses told them to "stand firm" and watch what God would do. What's the difference between panicking in a crisis and trusting God in a crisis? What helps you trust God when you're afraid?

4. **After crossing the sea, Moses and Miriam led the people in singing and dancing.** Why do you think worship was their immediate response? How can celebrating what God has done strengthen our faith?

5. **The song in Exodus 15 celebrates who God is, what he's done, and what he will do.** If you were to write a song about God based on your own life, what would you include?

The night had begun with death. It ended with deliverance. A nation of slaves had become a nation of free people. A lamb had died so that sons could live. A sea had parted so that the redeemed could walk through. And on the far shore, they sang.

But freedom was only the beginning. The Israelites had been saved *from* something—slavery in Egypt. Now they needed to learn what they had been saved *for*. The wilderness was waiting. And so was Mount Sinai.

Turn the page.

6

LEARNING TO TRUST

In *Finding Nemo*, Marlin spends the entire movie trying to rescue his son. He battles jellyfish, escapes sharks, survives an anglerfish, and crosses the entire ocean. Finally, against all odds, he finds Nemo in a dentist's fish tank in Sydney, Australia.

But here's the thing: the movie doesn't end when Marlin finds Nemo. There's still a whole final act. Nemo escapes the tank, reunites with his dad—and then they have to get home. The journey isn't over just because the rescue happened. In fact, some of the hardest lessons come after the reunion, when Marlin has to learn to trust Nemo and let go of his fear.

The same thing happens in Exodus. The Israelites have been rescued. They've walked through the Red Sea on dry ground. They've watched their enemies destroyed. They've sung songs of celebration on the far shore.

But now what? Now comes the journey. Now comes the wilderness. Now comes the long, hard process of learning to trust the God who saved them.

THREE DAYS WITHOUT WATER

The celebration at the Red Sea was barely over when reality set in. Moses led the Israelites away from the sea and into the Desert of Shur. For three days they traveled—and found no water.

Think about that. Thousands upon thousands of people. Children. Elderly. Livestock. In the desert. For three days. Without water.

When they finally arrived at a place called Marah, they were desperate. They could see the water. They could almost taste it. But when they tried to drink it, they spit it out. The water was bitter—contaminated with minerals that made it undrinkable. Marah means "bitter" in the original language. The name fit.

The people grumbled against Moses: "What are we to drink?" It's a fair question. They were in real trouble. But notice how quickly they went from singing praise by the sea to complaining in the desert. Three days. That's all it took for the songs to stop and the grumbling to start.

BITTER MADE SWEET

Moses didn't have an answer. But he knew who did. He cried out to the Lord, and the Lord showed him a piece of wood. Moses threw it into the water, and the water became drinkable—sweet instead of bitter.

We don't know how this worked. The text doesn't explain the science. It was a miracle, plain and simple. God transformed something undrinkable into something life-giving.

But God wasn't just solving a water crisis. He was teaching a lesson. "If you listen carefully to the voice of the LORD your

God and do what is right in his eyes," God said, "if you pay attention to his commands and keep all his decrees, I will not bring on you any of the diseases I brought on the Egyptians, for I am the LORD, who heals you."

God was testing them—not to make them fail, but to train them. The wilderness wasn't punishment. It was school. God was teaching his people to trust him, to obey him, to look to him for everything they needed.

After Marah, they came to Elim—a place with twelve springs of water and seventy palm trees. An oasis. Plenty of water, plenty of shade. God was providing. But more tests were coming.

HUNGRY AND COMPLAINING

About six weeks after leaving Egypt, the Israelites arrived in the Desert of Sin. (That's the name of the place, not a commentary on their behavior—though it might as well have been.) By now, they had run out of food. And the complaining got worse. "If only we had died by the LORD's hand in Egypt!" they said. "There we sat around pots of meat and ate all the food we wanted, but you have brought us out into this desert to starve this entire assembly to death."

Read that again. They actually said it would have been better to die in Egypt. This is what fear does. This is what hunger does. It makes you forget. The Israelites had been slaves—beaten, oppressed, their babies thrown into the Nile. But now that they were hungry, they remembered Egypt as a paradise of pots of meat and plenty of food. They were so focused on what they didn't have that they forgot what God had already done.

BREAD FROM HEAVEN

God's response to their complaining wasn't anger—at least not yet. It was provision. "I will rain down bread from heaven for you," God told Moses. "The people are to go out each day and gather enough for that day. In this way I will test them and see whether they will follow my instructions."

That evening, quail covered the camp—meat for dinner. And in the morning, when the dew lifted, there was something strange on the ground: thin flakes, white like frost, covering the desert floor.

The Israelites looked at it and said, "What is it?" They had never seen anything like it.

Moses told them, "It is the bread the LORD has given you to eat."

They called it manna—which basically means "What is it?" For the next forty years, this mysterious bread from heaven would be their daily food.

THE MANNA RULES

But manna came with rules. Each person was to gather only what they needed for that day—about two liters per person. No stockpiling. No hoarding. No taking extra "just in case."

Some people didn't listen. They gathered extra and saved it overnight. By morning, it was full of maggots and smelled terrible. The manna couldn't be stored.

Why would God design it this way? Because he was teaching them something crucial: they couldn't save up security for tomorrow. They couldn't build a stockpile that would make them independent of God. Every single day, they had to go out and gather. Every single day, they had to trust that God would provide again.

This was hard for former slaves. In Egypt, they had nothing that was truly their own. Now they were free—but freedom didn't mean they could hoard resources and rely on themselves. Freedom meant learning to depend on God daily.

But there was one exception. On the sixth day, they were to gather twice as much—enough for two days. Because on the seventh day, the Sabbath, no manna would appear. On that day, unlike every other day, the extra manna didn't spoil. It stayed fresh.

Some people went out on the seventh day anyway, looking for manna. They found nothing. God was frustrated: "How long will you refuse to keep my commands?"

The Sabbath wasn't optional. God was teaching them a rhythm of work and rest, of gathering and trusting. Six days you work; the seventh day you rest. And you trust that God has already provided what you need.

The manna would continue for forty years—until the day the Israelites entered the Promised Land and ate food from Canaan for the first time. An entire generation would grow up knowing no other food. Every morning of their lives would begin with walking outside and gathering what God had provided the night before.

WATER FROM A ROCK

More traveling. More desert. More problems. At a place called Rephidim, there was no water—again. And this time, the grumbling turned ugly. "Why did you bring us up out of Egypt to make us and our children and livestock die of thirst?" they demanded.

Moses was at his breaking point. "What am I to do with these people?" he asked God. "They are almost ready to stone me." God told Moses to take his staff—the same staff he had used to strike the Nile, the same staff he had raised over the Red Sea—and strike a rock at Horeb. Moses obeyed.

Water gushed out of the rock. Enough for everyone. Enough for the livestock. Life-giving water from solid stone. Moses named the place Massah and Meribah, which mean "testing" and "quarreling." Because that's what the people did there—they tested God and quarreled with Moses. They asked, "Is the LORD among us or not?" After everything they had seen—the plagues, the Passover, the parted sea—they still asked, "Is God really with us?"

ATTACK!

As if hunger and thirst weren't enough, the Israelites faced a new threat: enemies. The Amalekites attacked. They didn't come for a fair fight—they targeted the weak, the stragglers, the people at the back of the line who couldn't keep up.

Moses sent Joshua (who appears here for the first time) to choose some men and fight. Meanwhile, Moses went to the top of a hill with the staff of God in his hand.

Something strange happened. As long as Moses held up his hands, the Israelites were winning. When his hands dropped, the Amalekites started winning. Moses' arms got tired. So Aaron and another man named Hur sat Moses on a rock and held up his arms for him—one on each side—until sunset. Joshua and his army won the battle.

This is a picture of spiritual warfare. The battle wasn't won just by swords. It was won by prayer, by intercession, by looking to God. And it was won by teamwork—Aaron and Hur holding up Moses when he couldn't hold himself up anymore.

God told Moses to write down what happened and make sure Joshua remembered it: "I will completely blot out the memory of Amalek from under heaven." The Amalekites had attacked God's people at their weakest. God would not forget.

A VISITOR WITH ADVICE

After all this—bitter water, manna, water from a rock, battle with the Amalekites—Moses had a visitor. Jethro, his father-in-law, came from Midian to see him. He brought Moses' wife Zipporah and their two sons, who had been staying with Jethro during the chaos of the plagues and exodus.

This was a reunion. Moses had spent forty years in Midian, married Jethro's daughter, raised his sons there. Jethro had been like a father to him. Now, after everything that had happened in Egypt, Moses finally got to see his family again.

When Moses told Jethro everything God had done—the plagues, the rescue from Pharaoh, the deliverance at the sea, the provision in the wilderness—Jethro was overjoyed.

"Praise be to the LORD," he said, "who rescued you from the hand of the Egyptians and of Pharaoh. Now I know that the LORD is greater than all other gods." This was a remarkable statement. Jethro had been a priest in Midian—a priest of other gods. But after hearing what God had done, he confessed that the LORD was supreme. He offered sacrifices to God and ate a meal with Moses and the elders of Israel.

Jethro had become a believer. The story of the exodus wasn't just for Israel—it was for the nations too. When people heard what God had done, they could respond in faith, just like Jethro did. But Jethro also noticed a problem.

WEARING YOURSELF OUT

The next day, Jethro watched Moses at work. From morning until evening, Moses sat as judge for the people. Anyone with a dispute came to Moses. Anyone with a question about God's will came to Moses. The line never ended.

"What you are doing is not good," Jethro told him. "You and these people who come to you will only wear yourselves out. The work is too heavy for you; you cannot handle it alone." Moses was trying to do everything himself. He was the judge, the teacher, the counselor, the decision-maker for over a million people. It was unsustainable.

Jethro had practical advice: "Select capable men from all the people—men who fear God, trustworthy men who hate dishonest gain—and appoint them as officials over thousands, hundreds, fifties, and tens. Have them serve as judges for the people at all times. The simple cases they can decide themselves; the difficult ones they bring to you." It was a system of shared leadership. Not everything had to go through Moses. Qualified people could handle most issues. Moses could focus on teaching God's laws and handling the hardest cases.

Moses listened. He did everything his father-in-law suggested. He chose capable leaders and appointed them over the people. The work got done. Moses didn't burn out. The people got the help they needed. Sometimes the wisest thing a leader can do is accept help.

WHAT THIS MEANS FOR US

First, the wilderness comes after salvation. The Israelites weren't wandering in the desert because God had abandoned them. They were there because God was training them. Sometimes the hardest seasons of life come after we've experienced God's deliverance—not because God is punishing us, but because he's teaching us to depend on him.

Second, daily trust is harder than dramatic rescue. It's one thing to watch God part the sea. It's another thing to trust him for bread every single day. The Israelites struggled with daily dependence. So do we. We want security, guarantees, control. God wants us to come to him every morning with open hands.

Third, complaining reveals what we really believe. When things got hard, the Israelites accused God of bringing them into the desert to die. Their grumbling showed that they didn't really trust his character. Our complaints often reveal the same thing—that we doubt God's goodness when circumstances get difficult.

Fourth, we need each other. Moses couldn't hold up his own arms. He needed Aaron and Hur. He couldn't judge all the cases. He needed other leaders. The Christian life isn't meant to be lived alone. We need people to hold us up, share the load, and help us keep going.

TALKING POINTS

1. **The Israelites went from singing by the Red Sea to complaining in the desert in just three days.** Why do you think it's so easy to forget what God has done when new problems arise? How can we fight the tendency to forget?

2. **God provided manna every day but wouldn't let them store it up.** What was he trying to teach them? How does this apply to the way we trust God in our daily lives?

3. **At Rephidim, the people asked, "Is the LORD among us or not?"—right after God had miraculously provided manna and quail.** Why do you think they still doubted God's presence despite all the evidence? When are you most tempted to question whether God is really with you, and what helps you remember that he is?

4. **When Moses' arms got tired, Aaron and Hur held them up.** Who are the people in your life who "hold up your arms" when you're exhausted or struggling? How can you be that person for someone else?

5. **Jethro noticed that Moses was wearing himself out trying to do everything alone.** Why is it sometimes hard to accept help or share responsibilities with others? What can we learn from Moses' willingness to listen to Jethro's advice?

The wilderness was hard. The Israelites complained about water, complained about food, doubted God's presence, and faced enemies who wanted to destroy them. But through it all, God provided. Bitter water made sweet. Bread from heaven every morning. Water from a rock. Victory in battle. The wilderness wasn't the end of the journey. It was preparation for what came next.

Mount Sinai was waiting. And at that mountain, God was about to do something that would change everything: he was going to make a covenant with his people.

Turn the page.

7

THE MOUNTAIN THAT SHOOK

In *The Chronicles of Narnia*, there's a moment when the children first hear about Aslan. "Is he—quite safe?" Susan asks about the great Lion. "Safe?" replies Mr. Beaver. "Who said anything about safe? 'Course he isn't safe. But he's good. He's the King, I tell you."

That conversation captures something important: the God we serve is not a tame god. He's not a comfortable cosmic buddy who exists to make us feel good. He is powerful beyond imagination, holy beyond comprehension, and dangerous to anyone who approaches him carelessly.

The Israelites were about to learn this lesson firsthand. Three months after leaving Egypt, they arrived at Mount Sinai. The same mountain where God had spoken to Moses from a burning bush. The same mountain where God had promised, "When you have brought the people out of Egypt, you will worship God on this mountain." The promise was being fulfilled. But what happened next would terrify them.

EAGLES' WINGS

Before the thunder and fire came, God spoke tender words to his people. Moses climbed the mountain, and God gave him a message to deliver: "You yourselves have seen what I did to Egypt, and how I carried you on eagles' wings and brought you to myself."

Think about that image for a moment. In the ancient world, people observed how mother eagles cared for their young. Eagle chicks stay in the nest for about a hundred days—completely helpless, completely dependent. When it's time to fly, the mother doesn't push them out and hope for the best. She hovers beneath them, ready to catch them on her wings if they fall.

That's what God had done for Israel. He had attacked Egypt like a fierce bird of prey, swooping down to rescue his vulnerable children. He had carried them through the wilderness, providing food and water and protection. He had brought them safely to himself. The exodus wasn't just about getting Israel out of Egypt. It was about getting Israel close to God.

THE PROPOSAL

Then God made an incredible offer. "Now if you obey me fully and keep my covenant, then out of all nations you will be my treasured possession. Although the whole earth is mine, you will be for me a kingdom of priests and a holy nation."

Treasured possession. Kingdom of priests. Holy nation. These weren't small promises. God was offering to make Israel his most prized treasure—not because they were better than other nations, but because he chose to love them. He was offering to make them a nation of priests, which meant they would have direct access to him. And he was offering to make them holy—set apart, different from every other nation on earth.

There was a condition: "If you obey me fully and keep my covenant." This wasn't salvation by works. God had already saved them. He had already brought them out of Egypt, already carried them on eagles' wings. The obedience wasn't to earn his love—it was to live in relationship with him.

Moses brought God's words to the people. Their response was unanimous: "We will do everything the LORD has said." They had no idea what they were agreeing to.

GET READY

God told Moses to prepare the people. In three days, the Lord himself would come down on Mount Sinai in the sight of all the people.

But there were strict rules. The people had to consecrate themselves—set themselves apart, wash their clothes, prepare their hearts. They had to be ready to meet with a holy God.

And there were boundaries. No one was allowed to touch the mountain. Not even the foot of it. Anyone who crossed the line—person or animal—would be put to death.

Why such extreme measures? Because God is holy. His presence is not something to approach casually. The boundaries weren't cruel restrictions—they were protection. An unholy people cannot survive the unfiltered presence of a holy God.

THE THIRD DAY

On the morning of the third day, everything changed. Thunder rumbled. Lightning flashed. A thick cloud covered the mountain. And then came a sound like a trumpet—so loud that everyone in the camp trembled.

Moses led the people out of the camp to meet with God. They stood at the foot of the mountain and looked up. What they saw was terrifying. Mount Sinai was covered in smoke because the Lord had descended on it in fire. The smoke billowed up like smoke from a furnace. The whole mountain trembled violently.

This wasn't a gentle worship service. This was raw, overwhelming, terrifying power. The ground was shaking. The air was filled with smoke and fire. The trumpet blast grew louder and louder. Then Moses spoke, and God answered him with thunder. The Creator of the universe had arrived.

THE VOICE FROM THE FIRE

And then God spoke. Not through Moses. Not through an angel. God himself spoke directly to the entire nation—every man, woman, and child heard his voice thundering from the mountain. "I am the LORD your God, who brought you out of Egypt, out of the land of slavery."

Before giving a single command, God reminded them who he was and what he had done. He was the God who had rescued them. Everything that followed was built on that foundation. Then came the Ten Commandments.

THE TEN WORDS

The Bible doesn't actually call these "the Ten Commandments" in the original language. It calls them "the Ten Words"—which is where we get the term "Decalogue." These weren't just rules;

they were the foundational words that would define Israel's identity as God's people.

The first four commandments were about Israel's relationship with God:

"You shall have no other gods before me." God alone deserves worship. No competitors. No alternatives. He had proven himself in Egypt—there is no god like the Lord. The gods of Egypt had been exposed as powerless. Only the Lord had the power to save.

"You shall not make for yourself an idol." Don't try to reduce God to an image. Don't try to control him or contain him. No statue, no picture, no object can capture who he is. The nations around Israel worshiped gods they could see and touch. Israel was called to worship a God who was beyond all physical representation.

"You shall not misuse the name of the LORD your God." God's name represents his character, his reputation, his identity. Treat it with reverence. Don't use it carelessly, falsely, or as a weapon.

"Remember the Sabbath day by keeping it holy." Work six days; rest one. This pattern was built into creation itself. The Sabbath was a gift—a reminder that life is more than productivity, that humans were made for rest and worship, not endless labor. Former slaves especially needed to hear this: you are not defined by your work.

The next six commandments were about relationships with other people:

"Honor your father and your mother." Respect the people God placed in authority over you. Family matters. This is the only commandment that comes with a specific promise: "so that you may live long in the land the LORD your God is giving you."

"You shall not murder." Human life is sacred. Every person is made in God's image. Taking a life unjustly is an assault on the Creator himself.

"You shall not commit adultery." Marriage is a covenant. Sexual faithfulness protects families, protects trust, protects the foundation of society.

"You shall not steal." Respect what belongs to others. Don't take what isn't yours.

"You shall not give false testimony against your neighbor." Tell the truth, especially when it matters most. Lies destroy relationships, communities, and justice.

"You shall not covet." Don't let your heart be consumed with wanting what others have—their house, their spouse, their possessions, their life. Coveting is the root of so many other sins. It starts in the heart and works its way out.

NOT A CHECKLIST

Here's something important to understand: the Ten Commandments weren't meant to be a minimal checklist. They weren't about finding the line between acceptable and unacceptable behavior and then staying just on the right side.

These were broad principles pointing toward the kind of life God wants for his people. "You shall not murder" doesn't just mean "don't kill someone." It means value human life. Don't harbor hatred. Don't destroy people with your words.

Jesus made this clear centuries later when he said that anyone who is angry with their brother is in danger of judgment (Matthew 5:21–22). The commandment against murder goes all the way to the heart.

The Ten Commandments describe what it looks like to love God completely and love your neighbor as yourself. They're not the minimum requirements—they're the direction markers pointing toward holiness.

TOO AFRAID TO LISTEN

When the people saw the thunder and lightning, heard the trumpet, and saw the mountain smoking, they were terrified. They trembled and stayed at a distance. "Speak to us yourself and we will listen," they begged Moses. "But do not have God speak to us or we will die." They couldn't handle it. The unfiltered presence of God was too much. They needed a mediator—someone to stand between them and this overwhelming, terrifying, holy God.

Moses' response was remarkable: "Do not be afraid. God has come to test you, so that the fear of God will be with you to keep you from sinning."

Don't be afraid—but let the fear of God stay with you. That sounds like a contradiction, but it isn't. The Israelites didn't need to be afraid that God would destroy them—he had just saved them. But they did need to maintain a healthy awe and reverence for who he is. The fear of God isn't terror that makes you run away; it's respect that shapes how you live.

The people remained at a distance. Moses approached the thick darkness where God was.

WHAT THIS MEANS FOR US

First, God is not tame. Mount Sinai reminds us that the God we worship is not a comfortable, domesticated deity who exists to meet our needs. He is the Creator of the universe, holy and powerful beyond our comprehension. We should approach him with reverence and awe.

Second, God's commands are built on God's grace. Before giving a single commandment, God reminded Israel what he had done for them: "I am the LORD your God, who brought you out of Egypt." Obedience is our response to salvation, not the means of earning it.

Third, the commandments point us toward love. Jesus summarized the entire law with two commands: love God with all your heart, and love your neighbor as yourself. The Ten Commandments show us what that love looks like in practice.

Fourth, we need a mediator. The Israelites couldn't approach God directly—they needed Moses to stand between them. This points forward to Jesus, who is the ultimate mediator between God and humanity. Through him, we can approach God's throne with confidence.

TALKING POINTS

1. **The Israelites were terrified when they experienced God's presence at Sinai.** What's the difference between being afraid of God and having a healthy "fear of God"? How should reverence for God affect the way we live?

2. **God described the Israelites as his "treasured possession," a "kingdom of priests," and a "holy nation."** These weren't titles they earned—they were given by grace. How does

it change the way you see yourself to know that God calls his people treasured and holy? What responsibilities come with that identity?

3. **God reminded Israel of what he had done for them before giving them commandments.** Why do you think it was important to start with grace before giving rules? How does remembering what God has done for us change how we respond to his commands?

4. **The Ten Commandments cover our relationship with God (commandments 1–4) and our relationships with others (commandments 5–10).** Why do you think loving God and loving people are so closely connected?

5. **The Israelites begged for a mediator because they couldn't handle God's direct presence.** How does Jesus fulfill this need for us today?

The mountain had shaken. The voice had thundered. The commandments had been given. Israel now knew what God expected of them. They had agreed to the covenant: "We will do everything the LORD has said."

But agreeing to obey and actually obeying are two very different things. And Israel was about to fail in a way no one saw coming. While Moses was on the mountain receiving more instructions from God, the people at the bottom were about to make a golden calf.

Turn the page.

8

THE DEAL IS SEALED

When you sign up for a sports team, you don't just show up and start playing. There's a process. You fill out forms. Your parents sign waivers. You agree to follow the team rules—show up to practice, respect the coach, wear the uniform, play fair. And then, once everything is official, you're on the team.

A covenant works the same way, but it's way more serious. In the ancient world, a covenant was more than a contract. It was a binding relationship—a promise sealed with sacrifice, blood, and a shared meal. Breaking a covenant wasn't like quitting a team. It was betrayal. It was life and death.

At Mount Sinai, God was inviting Israel into a covenant relationship. They had heard the Ten Commandments thundering from the mountain. They had agreed to obey. But the covenant wasn't official yet.

Now it was time to seal the deal.

MORE THAN TEN

The Ten Commandments were the foundation—the big

principles that defined Israel's relationship with God and each other. But living in community requires more than ten rules.

What happens when someone's ox injures a neighbor? What about theft? What about property disputes? How should the Israelites treat the poor? How should they handle dangerous situations? What does justice look like when things go wrong?

God didn't leave them to figure this out on their own. After the Ten Commandments, he gave Moses a whole collection of laws and guidelines that scholars call "the Book of the Covenant." This section of Exodus (chapters 21–23) covers everything from how to treat servants to what to do if someone digs a pit and an animal falls in.

Some of these laws might seem strange to us today. We don't own oxen, and our legal system works differently. But the principles behind them still matter: protect the vulnerable, treat people fairly, take responsibility for your actions, and create a community where everyone can flourish.

PROTECTING THE WEAK

One thing that stands out in these laws is how much God cares about people who could easily be taken advantage of. Remember, the Israelites had been slaves. They knew what it was like to be powerless, to be mistreated, to have no one defend them. Now God was telling them: Don't do that to others.

"Do not mistreat or oppress a foreigner," God commanded, "for you were foreigners in Egypt."

"Do not take advantage of the widow or the fatherless. If you do and they cry out to me, I will certainly hear their cry."

"If you lend money to one of my people among you who is needy, do not treat it like a business deal; charge no interest." These laws created a society where the powerful couldn't crush the weak. Where strangers were welcomed instead of exploited. Where the poor weren't trapped in cycles of debt. Where widows and orphans had protection. God was building a different kind of nation—one that reflected his character.

JUSTICE, NOT REVENGE

The Book of the Covenant also includes a principle that sounds harsh at first: "Eye for eye, tooth for tooth, hand for hand, foot for foot." This might sound like permission for brutal revenge. But actually, it's the opposite.

In the ancient world, if someone from one family injured someone from another family, feuds could spiral out of control. You hurt my brother? I'll kill your whole family. Violence escalated without limit.

"Eye for eye" put a boundary on punishment. The penalty couldn't be worse than the crime. If someone knocked out your tooth, you couldn't kill them for it. Justice had to be proportional.

This was actually a step toward mercy—limiting revenge rather than encouraging it. And centuries later, Jesus would take it even further, teaching his followers to turn the other cheek and love their enemies.

SABBATH AND FESTIVALS

The laws weren't just about resolving conflicts. They also established a rhythm of life centered on worship.

Every seventh day: rest. The Sabbath wasn't just for Israelites—even servants and animals got a day off. God wanted his people to remember that life is more than work.

Every seventh year: let the land rest. Don't plant or harvest. Let the poor gather whatever grows on its own. Trust God to provide.

And three times a year, the Israelites were to gather for festivals: The Festival of Unleavened Bread—remembering the exodus from Egypt. The Festival of Harvest—celebrating the first crops. The Festival of Ingathering—thanksgiving at the end of the harvest.

These weren't optional. They were built into the calendar, ensuring that worship and gratitude and community remained central to Israel's identity. They would never be too busy for God.

THE PROMISE OF GUIDANCE

At the end of the Book of the Covenant, God made a promise: "See, I am sending an angel ahead of you to guard you along the way and to bring you to the place I have prepared." Israel wasn't going to wander into the Promised Land alone. God would guide them, protect them, fight for them. But there was a condition: "Pay attention to him and listen to what he says. Do not rebel against him."

This was the pattern of the covenant. God promised blessing and protection. Israel promised obedience and faithfulness. Both sides had responsibilities. If Israel obeyed, God would be an enemy to their enemies. He would drive out the nations before them. He would bless their food and water and take away sickness. But if they worshiped other gods or adopted the practices of the Canaanites, they would face the consequences.

The choice was theirs.

"WE WILL DO EVERYTHING"

Moses came down the mountain and told the people everything God had said—all the laws, all the instructions, all the promises and warnings. Their response was unanimous: "Everything the LORD has said we will do."

It's easy to say yes when you're standing at the foot of a mountain that's still smoking, when God's presence is fresh and terrifying, when the memory of your miraculous rescue is only three months old. Keeping that promise would be another matter entirely.

BLOOD OF THE COVENANT

The next morning, Moses built an altar at the foot of the mountain and set up twelve stone pillars—one for each tribe of Israel. Young men offered burnt offerings and fellowship offerings to the Lord.

Then Moses did something that might seem strange to us: he took half the blood from the sacrifices and splashed it against the altar. The other half he collected in bowls. He read the Book of the Covenant out loud to the people. Again they responded: "We will do everything the LORD has said; we will obey."

Then Moses took the blood from the bowls and sprinkled it on the people. "This is the blood of the covenant," he said, "that the LORD has made with you in accordance with all these words."

Blood sealed the covenant. It represented life—and the seriousness of death. The sacrificed animals died in place of the people. The blood sprinkled on the altar (representing God) and on the people bound them together in a sacred relationship.

Centuries later, Jesus would echo these words at the Last Supper: "This is my blood of the covenant, which is poured out for many for the forgiveness of sins." The new covenant would also be sealed with blood—but this time, the blood of God's own Son.

DINNER WITH GOD

After the covenant was sealed, something extraordinary happened. Moses and Aaron, Aaron's sons Nadab and Abihu, and seventy elders of Israel climbed the mountain. And there, they saw God. The Bible doesn't describe God himself—only what was under his feet: "something like a pavement made of lapis lazuli, as bright blue as the sky."

These seventy-four men saw God—and lived. Usually that was impossible. But God didn't strike them down. Instead, he welcomed them. "They saw God, and they ate and drank." A meal. In God's presence. On the holy mountain. This was a covenant meal, celebrating the relationship that had just been established. Like a wedding reception or a team dinner, it marked the beginning of something new. God and his people, together.

FORTY DAYS IN THE CLOUD

But God wasn't finished with Moses yet. "Come up to me on the mountain and stay here," God said. "I will give you the tablets of stone with the law and commandments I have written for their instruction." Moses told the elders to wait for him. He put Aaron and Hur in charge of handling any disputes. Then he and his assistant Joshua headed up the mountain.

When Moses reached the summit, the cloud of God's glory covered the mountain. For six days Moses waited in the cloud. On the seventh day, God called to him from within it. To the Israelites watching from below, the glory of the Lord on top of the mountain looked like a consuming fire.

Moses entered the cloud and stayed on the mountain for forty days and forty nights. That's a long time to wait at the bottom of a mountain, wondering if your leader is ever coming back. Long enough for people to get impatient. Long enough for them to forget their promises. Long enough for them to make a very, very foolish decision.

WHAT THIS MEANS FOR US

First, God cares about everyday life. The Book of the Covenant covers everything from worship to property disputes to caring for animals. Nothing is outside God's concern. He wants his people to reflect his character in the big things and the small things—in how we worship and how we treat our neighbors.

Second, covenants are serious. This wasn't a casual agreement. It involved sacrifice, blood, and binding commitment. When God makes promises, he keeps them. And when we make commitments to God, we should take them seriously.

Third, God wants relationship, not just rules. The laws were important, but they led to something bigger: a meal with God on the mountain. The goal was never just obedience—it was fellowship. God wanted to be with his people.

Fourth, our covenant is sealed with better blood. The animal sacrifices at Sinai pointed forward to Jesus. His blood established a new covenant—one that doesn't just cover sins temporarily but takes them away permanently. When we take communion, we're participating in the same kind of covenant meal the elders shared on Sinai.

TALKING POINTS

1. **The Book of the Covenant includes many laws about protecting foreigners, widows, orphans, and the poor.** Why do you think God emphasized caring for vulnerable people? How can we apply this today?

2. **"Eye for eye, tooth for tooth" was actually a limit on revenge—the punishment couldn't be worse than the crime.** Later, Jesus taught his followers to go even further and turn the other cheek. How do you see God's laws as steps that move people toward greater mercy over time? What does this teach us about how God works with people where they are while also calling them to something better?

3. **The Israelites twice said "We will do everything the LORD has said."** Do you think they fully understood what they were promising? Why is it easier to make commitments than to keep them?

4. **The elders saw God and ate a meal in his presence.** What does this tell us about what God wants with his people? How is this connected to communion today?

5. **Moses was on the mountain for forty days.** Why do you think God kept him there so long? What do you think the people below were thinking and feeling during that time?

The covenant was sealed. The meal was eaten. The stone tablets were being prepared. Everything seemed to be going perfectly. But down at the bottom of the mountain, the people were getting restless. Moses had been gone for over a month. Maybe he wasn't coming back. Maybe they needed a god they could see. The golden calf was about to be born.

Turn the page.

9

THE WORST MISTAKE

In *Frozen*, Elsa has a gift—the power to create ice and snow. But when fear takes over at her coronation, everything spirals out of control. She accidentally freezes her entire kingdom, runs away in shame, and nearly destroys her relationship with her sister Anna forever. One moment of panic. One terrible decision. And suddenly everything is in danger of falling apart.

The Israelites were about to have their Elsa moment. Moses had been on the mountain for over a month, meeting with God, receiving instructions for how to build a special dwelling place where God would live among his people. Everything was going according to plan. The covenant had been sealed. The stone tablets with the Ten Commandments had been written by God's own finger. And then, at the base of the mountain, the people made the worst mistake in Israel's history.

"MAKE US GODS"

The people got impatient. Moses had been gone for forty days. Forty days of staring at the smoking mountain. Forty days of wondering if their leader was ever coming back. Forty days with no visible evidence that God was still with them.

So they went to Aaron—Moses' brother, the same Aaron who had stood before Pharaoh, who had held up Moses' arms during battle, who had climbed the mountain and eaten a meal in God's presence. "Come, make us gods who will go before us," they said. "As for this fellow Moses who brought us up out of Egypt, we don't know what has happened to him."

They wanted something they could see. Something they could touch. Something that would guarantee God's presence on their terms, under their control. And Aaron—incredibly, unbelievably—said yes.

THE GOLDEN CALF

"Take off the gold earrings that your wives, your sons, and your daughters are wearing," Aaron told them, "and bring them to me." The people did it. They stripped off their jewelry and handed it over. Aaron melted the gold, shaped it with tools, and made it into an idol cast in the shape of a calf—or more accurately, a young bull.

Why a bull? Because that's what the Egyptians worshiped. After all those plagues that humiliated Egypt's gods, after walking through the Red Sea on dry ground, after everything God had done to prove he was greater than any idol—the Israelites went right back to Egyptian-style religion.

When the golden calf was finished, the people said, "These are your gods, Israel, who brought you up out of Egypt." This was insane. A statue they had just made with their own hands out of their own jewelry—and they claimed it had rescued them from slavery?

But Aaron wasn't done. He built an altar in front of the calf and announced, "Tomorrow there will be a festival to the LORD." He tried to combine idol worship with the worship of the true God. He put the Lord's name on a pagan ritual. And the next day, the people offered sacrifices, ate and drank, and "got up to indulge in revelry"—which is the Bible's way of saying the party got completely out of control.

"LET ME DESTROY THEM"

Up on the mountain, God knew exactly what was happening. "Go down," he told Moses, "because your people, whom you brought up out of Egypt, have become corrupt." Notice the language. God said "your people"—as if distancing himself from them. He was furious. "They have been quick to turn away from what I commanded them. They have made themselves an idol cast in the shape of a calf. They have bowed down to it and sacrificed to it."

Then came the terrifying words: "Now leave me alone so that my anger may burn against them and that I may destroy them. Then I will make you into a great nation." God was ready to end it. Wipe out the entire nation. Start over with Moses, just like he had once started over with Noah.

MOSES FIGHTS FOR ISRAEL

This was Moses' moment. He could have agreed. He could have stepped aside and let God pour out his wrath. After all, the people had complained about him constantly. They had doubted him. They had made his life miserable.

Instead, Moses fought for them. "LORD," he said, "why should your anger burn against your people, whom you brought out of Egypt with great power and a mighty hand?" He reminded God that these were his people—the ones God had rescued, not Moses.

"Why should the Egyptians say, 'It was with evil intent that he brought them out, to kill them in the mountains'? Turn from your fierce anger; relent and do not bring disaster on your people." He appealed to God's reputation among the nations.

"Remember your servants Abraham, Isaac, and Israel, to whom you swore by your own self: 'I will make your descendants as numerous as the stars in the sky.'" He appealed to God's promises.

And then—one of the most remarkable statements in the entire Bible: "The LORD relented and did not bring on his people the disaster he had threatened." God listened to Moses. He changed his course of action. Moses' intercession saved the nation from destruction.

THE TABLETS SHATTERED

Moses came down the mountain carrying the two stone tablets—the ones written by God himself. Joshua met him partway down and heard the noise from the camp. "There's the sound of war in the camp," he said. Moses knew better. "It's not the sound of victory or defeat. It's the sound of singing."

When Moses got close enough to see the calf and the dancing, his anger exploded. He threw the tablets and shattered them at the foot of the mountain. The covenant was broken—literally. The tablets that represented Israel's agreement with God lay in pieces on the ground, just like their faithfulness.

Moses burned the golden calf, ground it to powder, scattered it on the water, and made the Israelites drink it. Then he turned to his brother. "What did these people do to you, that you led them into such great sin?"

Aaron's excuse was pathetic: "You know how prone these people are to evil. They said, 'Make us gods.' So I told them, 'Whoever has any gold, take it off.' Then they gave me the gold, and I threw it into the fire, and out came this calf!" As if the calf had magically appeared on its own. As if Aaron had nothing to do with it.

THE COST OF SIN

Moses stood at the entrance to the camp and called out: "Whoever is for the LORD, come to me." The Levites—his own tribe—rallied to him. Moses gave them a terrible command: go through the camp with swords and execute those who refused to repent. About three thousand people died that day.

Sin has consequences. The Israelites had broken the first two commandments within weeks of receiving them. They had betrayed the God who saved them. And while God had shown mercy by not destroying the entire nation, there was still a price to pay.

"BLOT ME OUT"

The next day, Moses went back up the mountain. He knew the people's sin was not fully dealt with. "Oh, what a great sin these people have committed!" he said to God. "They have made themselves gods of gold. But now, please forgive their sin—but if not, then blot me out of the book you have written." Moses offered his own life for his people. He was willing to give up everything—even his place in God's eternal record—if it would save them.

God didn't accept the offer. But he did continue to show mercy. "Whoever has sinned against me I will blot out of my book," he said. "Now go, lead the people to the place I spoke of." The journey would continue. But everything had changed. God told Moses he would send an angel before them, but he himself would not go with them. "You are a stiff-necked people. If I were to go with you even for a moment, I might destroy you."

When the people heard this, they mourned. The worst consequence of their sin wasn't punishment—it was distance from God.

"SHOW ME YOUR GLORY"

What follows is one of the most intimate conversations in the Bible. Moses pleaded with God not to abandon them. "If your Presence does not go with us, do not send us up from here."

God agreed. "I will do the very thing you have asked, because I am pleased with you and I know you by name."

Emboldened, Moses asked for more: "Now show me your glory."

God's response was gracious but careful. "I will cause all my goodness to pass in front of you, and I will proclaim my name, the LORD, in your presence. … But you cannot see my face, for no one may see me and live."

God hid Moses in a cleft of the rock, covered him with his hand, and passed by. Moses saw God's back—as much of God's glory as a human could survive.

And as God passed, he proclaimed his own name: "The LORD, the LORD, the compassionate and gracious God, slow to anger, abounding in love and faithfulness, maintaining love to thousands, and forgiving wickedness, rebellion and sin." This is who God is. Even after Israel's terrible betrayal. Even after the golden calf. Compassionate. Gracious. Slow to anger. Forgiving.

But God also added: "Yet he does not leave the guilty unpunished." Grace and justice. Mercy and holiness. Both are true about God.

COVENANT RENEWED

God gave Moses new tablets—the covenant restored. Moses stayed on the mountain another forty days, and when he came down, his face was radiant. It literally glowed from being in God's presence. The people were afraid to come near him. Moses had to wear a veil when he talked to them, removing it only when he went back to speak with God.

The covenant was renewed. The relationship was repaired. But it would never be quite the same. The people had learned that sin has consequences—and that God's mercy is greater than they could ever deserve.

WHAT THIS MEANS FOR US

First, idolatry is trading the real God for a fake one. The Israelites didn't think they were rejecting God   they thought they were worshiping him through the calf. But you can't worship the true God through false means. Any time we try to make God into something we can control or manipulate, we've created an idol.

Second, leaders can fail spectacularly. Aaron should have known better. He should have stood firm. Instead, he caved to pressure and led the people into disaster. Even good people can make terrible choices.

Third, intercession matters. Moses stood between God's wrath and the people's sin. He pleaded for mercy. And God listened. This points forward to Jesus, who stands before God on our behalf, interceding for us.

Fourth, God is both just and merciful. He doesn't pretend sin doesn't matter. But he also doesn't abandon his people. The same God who punishes sin is the God who forgives wickedness, rebellion, and sin.

TALKING POINTS

1. **The Israelites got impatient waiting for Moses and decided to take matters into their own hands.** When have you been tempted to stop waiting on God and do things your own way? What happened?

2. **Aaron gave in to pressure from the people instead of standing firm.** What makes it hard to do the right thing when everyone around you is doing the wrong thing?

3. **Moses offered to give up his own place in God's book to save the people.** What does this tell us about what it means to truly love others? How does this point to what Jesus did for us?

4. **God described himself as "compassionate and gracious, slow to anger, abounding in love and faithfulness."** How does this description change or confirm what you already believed about God?

5. **When Moses came down from meeting with God, his face was so radiant that the people were afraid to come near him.** What does it look like for us to spend time with God in ways that change who we are? How might others notice the difference when we've been close to God?

The tablets were restored. The covenant was renewed. God would continue with his people. But before they could move forward, they had work to do. God had given Moses detailed instructions for building something special—a tent where God himself would dwell among them. It was time to build the tabernacle.

Turn the page.

10

A PLACE TO CALL HOME

In *E.T. the Extra-Terrestrial*, there's a scene where Elliott helps E.T. build a makeshift communication device so he can "phone home." It's cobbled together from ordinary stuff—a Speak & Spell, a coffee can, a coat hanger, some wires—but it becomes something extraordinary: a connection point between Earth and somewhere far beyond. A way for two worlds to meet.

The tabernacle was something like that—except God was the one building the connection. Think about what the Israelites had been through. Generations of slavery in Egypt. The terrifying plagues. The desperate escape through the Red Sea. Months of wandering in a harsh wilderness with no permanent home. The overwhelming experience at Mount Sinai, with thunder and lightning and a voice from the fire that was so terrifying they begged Moses to speak to them instead.

Through all of it, God had been with them—in the pillar of cloud by day and fire by night. But where exactly was God? How could they know he was near? How could they approach him? Where could they go to meet with him?

God's answer was the tabernacle—a portable dwelling place where the Creator of the universe would make his home right in the middle of their camp. Not a distant God on a mountaintop, but a present God in their neighborhood. A place where heaven and earth could meet.

"I WILL DWELL AMONG THEM"

While Moses was on the mountain for forty days, God gave him detailed instructions for a building project unlike any other. "Have them make a sanctuary for me," God said, "and I will dwell among them."

That single sentence is the heart of the entire tabernacle. God wanted to live with his people. Not just visit them occasionally. Not just speak to them from a distance. He wanted to pitch his tent in the center of their camp and be their neighbor.

The word "tabernacle" means "dwelling place" or "tent." God was going to have a tent—just like the Israelites had tents. When they moved, he would move. When they camped, he would camp. He was committing to be with them wherever they went.

But there was a problem. God is holy—completely pure, completely perfect, completely set apart. The Israelites were not. How could a holy God live among sinful people without destroying them? The tabernacle was designed to solve that problem. Every detail—the materials, the layout, the furniture, the rituals—pointed to how sinful humans could safely approach a holy God.

THE FREEWILL OFFERING

God could have snapped his fingers and made the tabernacle

appear out of thin air. Instead, he invited the people to participate. "Tell the Israelites to bring me an offering," God said. "You are to receive the offering for me from everyone whose heart prompts them to give." This wasn't a tax. It wasn't mandatory. It was a freewill offering—gifts given voluntarily, from the heart.

And the people responded with astonishing generosity. They brought gold, silver, and bronze. They brought blue, purple, and scarlet yarn. They brought fine linen and goat hair and animal skins. They brought precious stones and olive oil and spices.

In fact, they brought so much that Moses eventually had to tell them to stop. "The people are bringing more than enough for doing the work the LORD commanded to be done." This is one of the only times in history that a building project had to turn away donations!

Why were they so generous? Because they understood what was at stake. God was going to live among them. Their offerings weren't going to some abstract cause—they were building a home for the God who had rescued them from slavery.

SKILLED WORKERS

Building the tabernacle required more than materials. It required craftsmen. God specifically called two men—Bezalel and Oholiab—and filled them with his Spirit "with wisdom, with understanding, with knowledge and with all kinds of skills." These weren't just construction workers. They were artists, metalworkers, weavers, and designers, all empowered by God's Spirit to create something beautiful.

Think about that. The same Spirit who hovered over the waters at creation now filled these workers to build God's dwelling place. Their hammering and stitching and carving were acts of worship, just as much as any song or prayer. Every person who contributed—whether they gave gold or wove fabric or carved wood—was participating in something sacred.

THE LAYOUT

Picture the tabernacle in your mind. First, there was a large rectangular courtyard, about 150 feet long and 75 feet wide, surrounded by a fence of white linen curtains. Inside that courtyard stood two important objects: a bronze altar for sacrifices and a bronze basin filled with water for the priests to wash.

At the far end of the courtyard was the tabernacle itself—a tent about 45 feet long and 15 feet wide. This tent was divided into two rooms. The first room was called the Holy Place. It contained three pieces of furniture: a golden lampstand that provided light, a table holding twelve loaves of bread (called the "bread of the Presence"), and a small golden altar where incense was burned.

The second room—separated from the first by a thick curtain—was called the Most Holy Place, or the Holy of Holies. This was the innermost sanctuary, the place where God's presence dwelt. It contained only one piece of furniture: the ark of the covenant.

THE ARK OF THE COVENANT

The ark was a wooden chest covered in gold, about four feet long and two feet wide. Inside it were the stone tablets of the Ten Commandments—the terms of God's covenant with Israel. Later, a jar of manna and Aaron's staff (which had miraculously budded) would also be placed inside.

On top of the ark was a golden lid called the "mercy seat" or "atonement cover." At each end of this lid stood a golden cherub (an angelic figure), with wings stretched up and forward, overshadowing the mercy seat.

This was the most sacred spot in all of Israel. God said, "There, above the cover between the two cherubim that are over the ark of the covenant law, I will meet with you." The space between the cherubim, above the mercy seat, was where heaven and earth met. It was God's throne on earth—the place where his presence dwelt among his people.

Think about what this meant. The same God who created galaxies and spoke the universe into existence chose to localize his presence in a specific spot—between two golden angels on a wooden box in a tent in the desert. Not because he's small, but because he wanted to be near.

Only one person could enter the Most Holy Place: the high priest. And he could only enter once a year, on the Day of Atonement, bringing blood from a sacrifice to sprinkle on the mercy seat. Without that blood, even the high priest would die.

The curtain separating the Holy Place from the Most Holy Place was thick—about four inches—and woven with cherubim. It was a constant reminder that access to God's presence was restricted. Sin had created a barrier that couldn't simply be ignored.

THE FURNITURE AND ITS MEANING

Every piece of furniture in the tabernacle taught something about God and salvation.

The **Bronze Altar** stood at the entrance of the courtyard. Before anyone could approach God, sacrifices had to be made. Animals died in the worshiper's place, their blood poured out as payment for sin. This altar taught that sin is serious—so serious that it requires death—and that God provides a way for sinners to be forgiven.

The **Bronze Basin** was where the priests washed before entering the tabernacle. It represented cleansing and purity. You couldn't serve a holy God with dirty hands.

The **Golden Lampstand** had seven branches and provided the only light inside the Holy Place (there were no windows). It represented God as the source of light and life. The priests had to tend the lamps constantly, making sure they never went out.

The **Table with Bread** held twelve loaves, one for each tribe of Israel. Fresh bread was placed there every Sabbath. It represented God's provision—he was the one who gave his people their daily bread.

The **Altar of Incense** stood just before the curtain separating the Holy Place from the Most Holy Place. Incense was burned there every morning and evening, and the fragrant smoke rose like prayers going up to God.

The **Ark and Mercy Seat** represented God's throne and his covenant faithfulness. The law was inside the ark, but the mercy seat covered it—a picture of grace covering the demands of the law.

THE PRIESTS

God chose Aaron (Moses' brother) and his sons to serve as priests. They were the only ones allowed to enter the tabernacle and perform its rituals.

The high priest wore special garments: a blue robe, a breastpiece with twelve precious stones (one for each tribe), and a golden plate on his forehead engraved with the words "HOLY TO THE LORD."

Before they could serve, the priests had to be consecrated—set apart for their holy work. They were washed with water, dressed in their sacred garments, anointed with oil, and sprinkled with the blood of sacrifices. The process took seven days.

The priests represented the people before God. When the high priest walked into the tabernacle wearing the breastpiece with the names of the twelve tribes, he was carrying all of Israel on his heart into God's presence.

BUILT EXACTLY AS COMMANDED

After the disaster of the golden calf and the renewal of the covenant, the people finally got to work. Exodus 35–39 describes the construction in detail. What's remarkable is how often the text repeats the phrase "as the LORD commanded Moses." Over and over, we read that the workers did exactly what God had specified.

This wasn't creativity time. This wasn't "let's improve on God's design." The tabernacle had to be built precisely according to God's pattern. Why? Because the pattern came from heaven itself. God showed Moses a model, and every detail mattered.

When all the work was finished, Moses inspected everything. "Moses saw that they had done it just as the LORD had commanded. So Moses blessed them."

THE GLORY FILLS THE TABERNACLE

The final chapter of Exodus describes the most important moment of all. On the first day of the first month—exactly one year after the Passover in Egypt—Moses set up the tabernacle. He put each piece of furniture in its place, arranged everything according to God's instructions, and completed the work.

Then it happened. "The cloud covered the tent of meeting, and the glory of the LORD filled the tabernacle." The same cloud that had led them out of Egypt, the same glory that had appeared on Mount Sinai—now it descended and filled the tabernacle. God had moved in.

The glory was so intense that Moses himself couldn't enter. Think about that. Moses, who had spoken with God face to face, who had seen God's back on the mountain, who had a face so radiant he had to wear a veil—even he couldn't go in. The Creator of the universe had taken up residence in the middle of the Israelite camp, and his presence was overwhelming.

But this wasn't meant to keep people away forever. The tabernacle was designed so that, through the proper sacrifices and rituals, the priests could enter. The system God established made it possible for sinful people to approach a holy God—not carelessly, not casually, but genuinely. The barrier was real, but so was the access.

From that point on, whenever the cloud lifted from the tabernacle, the Israelites would pack up and follow it. When the cloud settled, they would stop and make camp. Day or night, in all their travels, the cloud of the Lord was with them.

God was home.

WHAT THIS MEANS FOR US

First, God wants to live with his people. The tabernacle wasn't God's idea of keeping his distance. It was his way of getting close. The holy God of the universe chose to pitch his tent among a bunch of former slaves in the middle of a desert. That's grace. **Second, sin creates a barrier that must be dealt with.** The elaborate system of sacrifices, washings, and rituals wasn't pointless ritual—it was necessary. A holy God cannot ignore sin. But he provided a way for his people to approach him safely. **Third, the tabernacle points to Jesus.** Jesus is the ultimate meeting place between God and humanity. He is the sacrifice that takes away sin. He is the high priest who represents us before God. He is the light of the world, the bread of life, the way into God's presence. When John wrote that "the Word became flesh and made his dwelling among us" (John 1:14), he used tabernacle language. Jesus "tabernacled" among us. **Fourth, we are now God's dwelling place.** The New Testament teaches that believers are the temple of the Holy Spirit (1 Corinthians 6:19). God doesn't live in buildings made with hands—he lives in his people. The church, collectively, is being built into "a dwelling in which God lives by his Spirit" (Ephesians 2:22).

TALKING POINTS

1. **The Israelites gave so generously that Moses had to tell them to stop.** What does their response teach us about giving? How does understanding what we're giving to (building a place for God to dwell) change our attitude toward generosity?

2. **God filled Bezalel and Oholiab with his Spirit to do artistic and craftsman work.** What does this tell us about how God views creative and practical skills? How might God want to use your unique talents and abilities for his purposes?

3. **Every piece of tabernacle furniture taught something about approaching God.** Which piece of furniture do you find most meaningful, and why?

4. **The glory of God filled the tabernacle so powerfully that even Moses couldn't enter.** What does this tell us about God's holiness? How does Jesus change our ability to approach God?

5. **God wanted to live among his people—in a tent, in their camp, moving when they moved.** What does this tell us about God's character and his desire for relationship with us?

The book of Exodus ends with the cloud of God's glory resting on the tabernacle and the people of Israel ready to continue their journey. They had been slaves. Now they were free. They had been lost. Now they had direction—the cloud would lead them. They had been far from God. Now he lived among them.

The exodus was complete. But the story was just beginning. Ahead lay the wilderness wanderings, the conquest of Canaan, the rise of kings, the building of the temple, the exile and return—and eventually, the coming of One who would be God's presence in human flesh. The tabernacle in the wilderness was just a shadow of better things to come. But for those Israelites standing in the desert, watching the glory of God descend on that tent of meeting, it was enough. God was with them.

And that made all the difference.